"Rhondalynn has a tremendous outlook on life. Her balanced view of human nature and its inner workings, combined with a great sense of humour, has made Rhondalynn a person that I immensely proud to know. Her drive, determination and passion are the main elements that make Rhondalynn a great author, speaker and motivator. Buy this book – her journey will inspire you!"

Kevin Maddox
ActionCOACH

"Rhondalynn is a powerful public speaker, author and motivator with an amazing ability to connect with people. Her philosophy is to give extra value to everyone, whether they be colleagues or clients - and she delivers every time! Her knowledge and experience in business, communication, influence and the science of the mind makes Rhondalynn the 'go to' person for anyone serious about transformation and acceleration of their business or personal life. The material in this book is a proverbial gold mine."

Dr. Martin Preston
ActionCOACH and Consultant Psychiatrist

"I have known Rhondalynn through a number of lives - over time I have grown to understand the diversity, depth and degree of her abilities. She is truly a remarkable business woman and problem solver. I am a better person and business man for knowing her and I highly recommend this book to anyone who is looking to take their results and lives to the next level."

Craig Missell
Owner, Match2 Personnel

"This book will strike chords deep in the hearts and minds of all of us. It is one of the best books ever written on the subject."

Ben Angel, Owner, Nationwide Networking

"I've never met anyone as passionate, committed, and authentic as Rhondalynn. She's one of the best! Doing what it takes to make our world and business communities more successful, powerful, and authentic."

Christopher Steely
Director of Support, ActionCOACH

ON THE SHOULDERS
of GIANTS

33 new ways to guide yourself to greatness

BY

RHONDALYNN KOROLAK

Cover Design by Chameleon Print Design
Cover photograph: iStock Photo
Author photograph: Yusuke Sato
Printed and bound in Australia by BookPOD

This book is available for purchase from:-
www.imagineeringunlimited.com
and
www.bookstore.bookpod.com.au

Library of Congress Control Number: 2008910915

ISBN: 978-0-9805578-0-0

Acknowledgements

In search of my mother's garden, I found my own. ~ Alice Walker

I started off on this epic journey of self-discovery some sixteen years ago after my mother was brutally murdered. I was desperate for answers. I spent many years searching for my mother's garden - trying to keep her memory alive, doing what I thought she wanted me to do and fighting for my right to be the victim.

Surprisingly somewhere along the way, I stumbled upon my own garden. The answers I was so desperate to find, found me. The surprise was not so much in what I found but rather where I found it. I discovered my own truths, my answers, my power, my meaning...and in so doing I set myself free and began living again.

This book represents a snapshot of the experiences and insights that have moulded and shaped me into the person I am today. These are true stories - real people doing the best they could in often impossible circumstances with the resources they had available at the time. In my mind, there are no villains and there is no judgment. I am sincerely grateful for all the lessons that I have been entrusted with and the many wise teachers and giants who have graced my life thus far.

Writing this book was an overwhelming and daunting task. I found that the words poured onto the page relatively easily but with them came vivid emotions and memories that I thought I had successfully buried. Had it not been for the support, encouragement, understanding and expertise of Karen McCreadie, this book simply would not have been possible. I consider it an absolute miracle that we connected via the internet and that she agreed to assist me with this project. I respect, trust and admire her immensely. She helped me to write the thoughts I couldn't express easily but desperately needed to communicate and she often read my mind and my heart - which was no easy task. I also wish to acknowledge Clare Hallifax for her hard work, dedication and contribution to the professional editing of this book.

Most of the real "gold" in this book, however, is not my own - I have been fortunate enough to meet some amazing mentors and teachers along my journey that have shown me the path when I had lost my way. Each and every one of them is an amazing individual and I owe them so much more than words can express - Nicholas and Alvina Kutinsky, Gary Kovacs, Sondra Goplen, Sonya Savage, Rhoda Dobler, Dianna Lynn, Debra Tate, Rachel Wilson, Harwant Riehl, Angela Gawne, Debbie Hardwick, Jackie Keeble, Jeff Poule, Grant Thomas, Josephine Brown, Kieran Perkins, Anthony Robbins, Justice John Rooke, Darwin Greaves, Rev. Sigmund Schuster, Roger Sept, Gary Anderson, Mrs. Styles, Dr. Dave McMullen and Rod Turnbull.

A special thank you goes out to my best friend Tabatha Neigum - who has always believed in and encouraged me. We have been through so much together over the years and I simply cannot imagine what my life would be like without her in it. She is the most beautiful, loving and genuine person - I am truly blessed to have met her and I am in awe of her strength and courage.

Most of all, this book is a tribute to the memory of my mother, Darlene Korolak. There is never a day goes by that I don't miss her, she truly was an amazing, gentle and caring woman. She was only forty three years old when she died - far too early for someone who was so vibrant and full of life. I take comfort in the fact that she is always with me - watching over me, guiding me and encouraging me to pursue my dreams and to stand up for what I believe in. This book is as much her accomplishment as it is mine.

Contents

Introduction

In 1159, theologian and author John of Salisbury wrote a treatise on logic called Metalogicon. Although written in Latin the gist of what Salisbury said is, *'We are like dwarfs sitting on the shoulders of giants. We see more, and things that are more distant, than they did, not because our sight is superior or because we are taller than they, but because they raise us up, and by their great stature add to ours'.*

Centuries later, in 1676, Isaac Newton sent a letter to his rival Robert Hooke. He wrote, *'What Descartes did was a good step. You have added much in several ways ... If I have seen a little further it is by standing on the shoulders of Giants'.*

This book is about the giants of life, the scientists, scholars, writers and philosophers that have positively influenced our understanding of the world and offered us new perspectives. These are the giants whose words litter personal developments books, whose wisdom is often spun to create self-help homilies about the all-abiding importance of a positive attitude.

But let's face it; having a positive attitude is easy when life is good. It's easy when you are already thinking happy thoughts to remember to always expect the best. It's easy when you're supported by a loving relationship, a fulfilling career or great friends to feel optimistic about life. It's easy for the quotes and snippets of wisdom to clearly resonate with your experiences, serving only to galvanize your positive disposition.

But what happens when the shit hits the fan? What happens when everything you know is ripped away from you? What happens when the love of your life runs off with your best friend, leaving you with three young children? What happens when you lose your job and your house gets repossessed? What happens when your marriage falls apart or your business goes down the tubes? What happens if you just hate your life and can't see any way to change it? What happens if you suffer from chronic illness or your child is diagnosed with a terminal disease? Or what happens if a loved one is killed before their time?

Does the wisdom of philosophers or scientists hold any weight then? Do the words of these giants really help when your world is engulfed by darkness?

Many of the most popular motivational speakers today would have us believe they can. Open any self-help book and you will find it is not uncommon for financial distress to be the driving force behind the personal transformation of many well-known speakers and authors. No doubt, living on the streets, eating only every third day or being $70,000 in debt could be the catalyst for enormous growth and change. Similarly, being 100lbs overweight or extremely frustrated in a dead-end career could be the turning point that gives someone crystal clarity about what they want to create in their life.

I don't want to poke fun at the personal development industry nor do I want to trivialise these issues – which I agree individually or collectively would be a source of significant dissatisfaction, pain and unhappiness. However, what I do want to talk about is a completely different level of pain, another kind of darkness entirely. I'm talking about the darkness that shuts you down completely. The empty, no-return, nothing will ever be the same again darkness, a cold, damp blanket of pain that seems sure to extinguish even the frailest ember or faintest whisper of hope. From a place of complete despair and senseless tragedy, is it possible to stand on the shoulders of giants and find hope and meaning again?

The answer is, 'Yes'.

Sometimes there are moments in life that instantly rip the past and the future apart. Everything is irrevocably divided into 'before' and 'after'. Life as you know it dissolves and an alien, foreign and unwelcoming world appears in its wake.

For me that moment was about 4 pm on April 14th in 1992. I was studying for my final law exams. I had just returned to my house from the law school library and the phone rang. It was the Dean of the Law School.

She asked me to sit down … my mother had been murdered. The Federal Police (RCMP) hadn't been able to find me on campus. Concerned that I would discover the awful truth from the TV news, the Dean had finally been forced to tell me over the phone. Shortly after the call, I saw the story on the national news. They had found her body in a ditch; she had been strangled, suffered multiple stab wounds and had been badly beaten.

My mum was Head of Histology at the municipal hospital; in the 25 years she'd worked there she had rarely taken sick leave or been late, so when she failed to show up for work, the alarm was raised. She had been murdered in her own home two days earlier by three 16-year-old boys. Those boys had been given a key to the house by my 18-year-old brother. On the promise of a $500 beaten-up truck as reward, they went to her home in the middle of the night and brutally murdered her. They rolled her bloody body in a rug, drove her to the countryside and dumped her in a ditch. The next day, the boys and my brother cleaned up the house and went shopping to pick out the things they would buy when the insurance money came through.

By the time I was told, the boys and my brother were already in jail. I was 24 years old and I had lost my family. When I saw her body, although I knew it was her, all I could recognise were her hands. I could never do justice with mere words to the magnitude of that event. I could never explain the searing pain, shock, disbelief and numbness that eclipsed my life for years following her death.

To lose such a loving parent was bad enough, but to do so at the instigation of my own brother was inconceivable. The loss and betrayal were collectively almost more than I could bear. I knew he unfairly blamed her for the end of my parents' marriage, and I had been worried by his open hostility towards her, but I never really believed he was capable of such atrocity. And yet as soon as I heard what had happened, I knew intuitively that he was involved. My mum's only real crime was marrying the wrong man, a man incapable of taking responsibility for his alcoholism and abuse and of fostering hatred in my brother.

I am by no means the only one to experience extreme trauma. Open any newspaper from Melbourne to London to New York or Tokyo and you'll read of some disaster that's fractured someone's life. A senseless killing that will haunt those connected for years.

Life's not always pretty. It's hard, it's messy and it's unpredictable. It's often stranger than fiction and it can break your heart. But as this book will attest, real life is also magnificent, beautiful and awe-inspiring. We each are a composite of the experiences and conditioning we grow up with. There is goodness and kindness all around us and we survive or prosper because we are able to stand on the shoulders of giants.

Giants can take the form of great philosophers and scientists, great presenters, poets and writers. Perhaps, more importantly, they can take the form of a good friend, a wise elder, a loving stranger or a protective teacher – everyday heroes who profoundly touch our lives and change its course without ever really knowing the gift they have given.

I am eternally grateful to the giants in my life, my grandparents, friends, famous scholars and the teachers who have given me a new perspective and genuinely changed my life. My hope is that this book will open your eyes to the profound wisdom of the giants in your own world, of the people who will reach out and help you when you can't walk another step, the people who care, even if they find it hard to express it in words. I hope it also reminds you of the instances where your actions have made you a hero or a giant to others and that it will encourage and inspire you to continue to do so.

I hope that the concepts and ideas so often hijacked by the self-help gurus truly come alive for you as fact, and you begin to see their relevance in your own life. Often these philosophical perspectives are many thousands of years old, they are born in science, truth and mysticism and sadly trivialised through psychobabble. I hope that you see their wisdom through fresh eyes and learn to apply their gifts.

But most of all, it is my sincere desire that this book affirms to you that it is not what happens to you that matters it's what you decide to do about it. It's about what you do and who you become because of what happens, not despite it.

Chapter 1

The finest steel goes through the hottest fire. ~ Richard Nixon

> Richard Milhous Nixon was the 37th President of the United States from 1969 to 1974 and was the only President to ever resign from office. More often remembered for his infamous involvement with the Watergate scandal, Nixon's administration wasn't all bad. Under his leadership the relationships between the US and the Soviet Union and the US and China were greatly improved.

You might consider it odd that I have chosen a disgraced US President as my first giant. And yet I have found huge comfort from his quote throughout the most difficult times in my life. His words pulled me back to a more balanced position when I felt overcome with sorrow and unsure if I could carry on.

I vividly remember reading the quote for the first time. It was about three years after my mother's death. Up until that point I had considered myself damaged goods. I couldn't see any other explanation for what had happened and I felt as though I was broken. I felt a deep sense of loneliness and shame – I felt there was obviously something deeply wrong with me to have come from a family where something so awful could happen. Life felt such a struggle, as though everything from that point forward was always going to be tainted and overshadowed by my past. I was going to have to 'survive' the rest of my life, not live it! And then I found eight little words ...

The finest steel goes through the hottest fire.

In an instant my whole perspective shifted. What if I wasn't broken by what happened but I was actually moulded by those events and something

15

strong, meaningful and positive could emerge as a result? We all have scars. Some of them may be visible to others through illness, accident or disability or they may be internal emotional scars that no one else knows about. Both can be debilitating. This simple little quote allowed me to see for the first time that I was who I was not despite losing my mum but because of it. I couldn't change the past no matter how much I wanted to but I could change 'right now' and by doing so I could certainly change my future. I realised in that moment that I actually had a distinct advantage over most people – I had already experienced the worst thing I could ever imagine … and survived! I felt sure that I could handle ANYTHING that life threw at me, because I already had.

People worry everyday about what's around the corner. It is so easy to get caught up in worrying about financial difficulties, illness, global events, or even our own mortality, that we often forget to dedicate any of our time and energy towards actually *living*. I am thankful every single day. I am thankful for the knowledge that no matter what happens, no matter what life brings my way – it will never break me!

Yes, I have scars, but they were not 'terminal' blemishes as I had once thought, they were not evidence of my defects or validation of my lack of worthiness. They were the result of the 'hottest fire' and they would empower me to emerge with the strength and unbending determination of 'the finest steel'. This quote was a simple reminder that life isn't easy but that perhaps it was never designed to be! That amazing things can happen, character and strength often develop through the most challenging of circumstances and whether the heat destroys you or sculpts you is entirely up to you.

I used to be frustrated and overwhelmed by all the obstacles and hardships that I encountered on the journey towards my ideal life. I saw these as hindrances that held me back and prevented me from really living my life to the fullest and achieving my potential. But then one day I realised that the trials and tribulations were my life. As Bette Howland once said, *For a long time it seemed to me that real life was about to begin, but there was always some obstacle in the way. Something had to be got through first, some unfinished business; time still to be served, a debt to be paid. Then life would begin. At last it dawned on me that these obstacles were my life.'* Day by day, the obstacles and challenges I faced were slowly bending, moulding and shaping me into the woman that I was truly meant to be.

Did you know … ?

American psychologists and authors Richard Bandler and John Grinder are best known as the inventors of Neuro-Linguistic programming (NLP) – an **interpersonal communication** model based on the subjective study of language, non-verbal communication and personal change. It wasn't until I discovered NLP that I realised what had actually happened the moment I read the Nixon quote. I had experienced what is called a re-frame.

Reframes are linguistic tools used to transform a person's perspective from the currently held belief to any number of different possible interpretations or meanings. We ascribe meaning or significance to every event that we experience. These meanings are then stored in the subconscious mind and recalled at a later date (as beliefs, memories or decisions) to support or corroborate what we believe to be true about ourselves and the world we live in. A re-frame is a way to interrupt the patterns we have forged by putting the idea, memory, belief or decision into a new and empowering context. In so doing, the idea, memory, belief or decision takes on an entirely different meaning and this opens the door to new and more resourceful choices.

Much like a small stick of dynamite, the reframe has the power to shake an idea, memory, belief or decision at its very foundation. Successful reframes can be delivered via precise questioning or statements which allow the individual to redefine a situation or memory so they can find an empowering meaning and move forward in their life.

Bandler and Grinder's contribution to personal transformation is enormous. They developed NLP by modelling three exceptional psychotherapists: Virginia Satir, Fritz Perls and Milton Erickson. Today the predominant patterns of NLP and its many variants are taught in seminars, workshops, books, exercises and audio programs of many famous speakers such as Anthony Robbins, Tad James, Brian Tracy, Tony Buzan and Christopher Howard.

Nixon was up to his neck in political espionage and sabotage; he abused his power and eventually paid the price. And yet in some way his quote is especially poignant to me because of the scandal, not despite it. As I learnt more about him I realised that whist he made mistakes (granted pretty big ones!) he also did some great things in his time as President.

He opened communication and worked to remove the tension in some key relationships, which were potentially explosive – for both sides.

I have experienced some incredibly challenging times in my life but I am not alone. There are millions of people the world over who have been forged by intense heat and pain. Those that have risen to meet the challenges they faced and fought to survive.

Lance Armstrong is a well-known and inspirational example. Diagnosed with advanced testicular cancer that had already spread to his lungs and brain, Armstrong was given a 50/50 chance of survival. But he did so much more than survive. He beat cancer and returned to the sport he loved, going on to win the Tour de France – the most gruelling cycle race on earth – an incredible seven times. Armstrong is quoted as saying that cancer was *'the best thing that ever happened to him'*. His best performance was made possible by his cancer, not despite it. He was able to use his fear and win the greatest battle of his life. And in so doing, he offered hope and inspiration to millions of others. His contribution to the world of cycling is undisputed but perhaps his greatest contribution is to the people affected by cancer every year.

Or what about the kids in Rwanda who were abducted from their families in the dead of night? Children as young as eight years old were kidnapped and forced into a life of unfathomable violence – how do you recover from such unspeakable horror? With the help of UNICEF, these kids are being rehabilitated, cared for and reintegrated back into their communities. They are excited at the prospect of going to school and are being helped to face their own demons and go on to live productive lives.

The idea expressed so poetically by Nixon has also been articulated by many others. For example, Friedrich Nietzsche said *'That which does not kill us makes us stronger'*. I've also heard, *'If God brought you to it, He'll bring you through it'*.

Learning to come to terms with all the parts of your life – even the hard bits – can be a liberating experience. If you had a 5-carat diamond ring given to you by your great grandmother and your house burnt down, would you walk away from the ash and rubble or would you get down on your hands and knees and look for it? Diamonds are forged through extreme circumstances and so are we. And no matter what disaster or difficulty you experience, by standing on the shoulders of giants, we can all find the diamonds – the magnificence of our true selves – in the ashes.

How to incorporate this wisdom into your life

Limited thinking is very pervasive – people will do and say almost anything to defend their limitations. Think about the last conversation you had with a work colleague over coffee or with that friend who just popped by to have a chat about the troubles they were having with their spouse. Did they use negative statements, limiting beliefs, reasons and excuses for why they couldn't do something? Did it sound convincing? Or were these statements and excuses simply the 'truth' or the 'facts' based on *their* interpretation of events? Is it possible that we could change our experience of events simply by finding a new or alternative interpretation? NLP says categorically, 'Yes, it is possible'.

So think of a belief, decision or behaviour that you have right now that is holding you back in some area of your life. It could be something similar to:

- I can't start my own business because I am a single parent.
- I will never be a successful because I didn't go to university.
- I will never be rich because my parent's didn't teach me how to manage money.
- I will never be a good parent because I came from a broken family.
- My child or spouse never listens to me and this means that they don't respect me.
- My spouse is a workaholic and this means they don't love me anymore.

Take your statement (or one you relate to from the list above) and ask yourself: *'What else could this mean?'* or *'What is it that I have not noticed within this particular situation that could expose a new possible meaning, and therefore change my response to the person or situation?'*

EXAMPLE

Comment: *I can't start my own business because I am a single parent.*

Reframe: Isn't it possible that the time and money management skills that you have mastered as a single parent will increase your chance of success as an entrepreneur? Isn't it possible that the responsibility you feel toward your children could be a driving force toward success in your new venture ensuring you maintain your motivation and sweep aside all and any challenges you meet? Isn't it possible that starting your own business could offer you a level of freedom and security that would ensure you were never at the mercy of an employer again and you could fit your work around you children making you an even better role model and parent?

EXAMPLE

Comment: *My spouse is a workaholic and this means they don't love me anymore.*

Reframe: Isn't it possible that the reason your partner is a workaholic is because they love you so much? They want you to have the very best money can buy? Perhaps all this means is that it's now time to discuss how you feel? Your partner may be relieved to hear that you would like them to take it easier and spend more time together – that the money isn't all that important to you.

Chapter 2

The Map is not the Territory ~ Alfred Korzybski

Alfred Korzybski was a Polish philosopher and scientist best remembered for his theory of general semantics. In essence Korzybski believed that we are limited in what we know by the structure of our nervous system and the structure of our language. Our experience of the world is therefore not necessarily an objective perspective but rather it is influenced by what our mind interprets and how we describe it.

If you have come in contact with Neuro-Linguistic Programming (NLP) you will probably have heard of this statement. But what does it actually mean? As the developer of general semantics, Korzybski was studying reality and it was obvious to him that what we presumed to be reality was only ever one representation or interpretation of what could be described as reality. The way he articulated this was by saying the map was not the territory and therefore there was no such thing as objective reality.

If you look at a map of Melbourne, it is only a representation of Melbourne. No matter how good the map, even if it shows every detail, even if the map was a full-scale model of Melbourne created down to the last lamppost, it is still just a map. It is a representation and not Melbourne itself. In life, our memory is our map. We use our memory, the cumulative experiences of our life, to influence our present terrain. We assume that the map is the terrain and that what we remember or what we believe about our past experience is the truth. Yet reality is not concrete. It is entirely subjective – based on the map we hold of the world.

That map is never accurate but we assume it is. It is this conflict of maps that causes so much of the conflict in the world. We wrongly assume that what we think is true or right or accurate is exactly that. And yet if you put two people of varying religious beliefs together they will both believe that their viewpoint is correct.

What we believe is real is nothing more than an interpretation and the words we use to describe that interpretation.

One day Korzybski was giving a lecture to a group of students and in the middle of the lesson he went to his briefcase to retrieve a packet of biscuits wrapped in white paper. He muttered that he had to eat something and asked the students in the front row if they would also like a biscuit. A few students took a biscuit and started eating. Korzybski says, 'Nice biscuit, don't you think', while he took a second one and the students were in the front row were happily munching away. He then tore off the white paper from the biscuits, in order to reveal the original packaging. On it was a big picture of a dog's head and the words 'Dog Cookies'.

The students were shocked and two ran out the lecture theatre with their hands over their mouths as though they were going to throw up. 'You see, ladies and gentlemen', Korzybski remarked, 'I have just demonstrated that people don't just eat food, but also words, and that the taste of the former is often outdone by the taste of the latter.' Apparently his prank aimed to illustrate how some human suffering originates not from reality itself but from the confused representations we make about reality. The reality was those students and Korzybski ate dog biscuits but that wasn't what made them sick. The same effect would have occurred if they were not dog biscuits but wrapped as though they were. The reality of the situation was irrelevant – whether they were dog biscuits or not was irrelevant to whether they became sick or not. The only difference was that one minute they *thought* they were eating a nice biscuit and in the next they *thought* they were eating a dog biscuit. The distress was only caused by their perceived reality.

This principal is particularly relevant in the context of examining where things might go wrong in relationships – either personal or business. Anytime you have more than one person observing an event, the door is open for the possibility of misinterpretation and miscommunication based on differing maps of reality. Learning to recognise that we all have different maps (filters by which we see and process the world around us) allows us to see the world through another person's eyes and therefore understand, relate and communicate with greater respect and results.

Years ago, in Canada, I was married for about seven years. In many ways my husband and I were really quite different from each other but we never identified or discussed those differences prior to getting married. Our family upbringings and experiences were disparate and we had diverse goals and ideas about what we wanted for our future. I was very emotional, spontaneous, laid back and a risk taker – I felt more comfortable flying by the seat of my pants. Tim, on the other hand, was an engineer – very level-headed, practical, organised, structured and methodical. His map of the world was entirely different to mine – everything had to be in its right place and major life decisions were planned out on paper well in advance, along with contingency and back-up plans.

A couple of years into the marriage, we began to discuss starting a family. I had met Tim about one year after my mother had passed away, so he had been with me through some really tough times and he knew that I really struggled with the fact that I had lost my immediate family. Even though I had always been very career-focused, I was open about the fact that I very much wanted to have a family of my own one day. I desperately wanted a chance to create a new family and a sense of belonging, connection and foundation. Tim's family was particularly welcoming to me and I really enjoyed the times when we would go to his parent's house for the holidays and we would be surrounded by his four siblings, their spouses and all their children. It was loud, hectic and pretty full on but there was a real sense of love and support.

I was still struggling with the loss of my mother and had tried many forms of counselling and therapy to help in my healing. The first real turning point for me came when I was referred to a psychiatrist, Dr Dave McMullen. I don't actually think he was many years older than me – he might have been 30 years old when I first met him and he was the most casual, laid-back guy you could ever meet. Whenever I went to his office, he would be there in khaki pants and a casual shirt looking more prepared for a mountain hike than a medical appointment. He was incredibly good at what he did and he had a way of making me feel very comfortable and accepted.

I saw him about once a month for more than two years. There wasn't much that we didn't talk about. He had seen me take great strides in dealing with the loss of my mother and I was genuinely beginning to feel much stronger. I remember very distinctly telling him one day that my husband wanted to meet him. Dave asked me why and I told him that, 'he has prepared a list of all of the things that are wrong with me. He feels that because my parents were divorced and I haven't properly dealt with the death of my mother, I am somehow damaged goods. He doesn't think I will make a good mother and he doesn't want to have children with me.'

What Dave said to me on that day changed my life forever. He said, 'I have no doubt that your husband needs to see a psychiatrist, but you, however, do not! There is nothing wrong with you – you are not broken. You have been through an unbelievably tough ordeal and you are coping extremely well. What you have done and who you have become, despite your upbringing and the loss of your mother is precisely the reason that I know you will make an incredible mother one day. You cannot let someone else's map of reality limit what you believe that you can do.'

At the end of the day, there was no right or wrong in this situation. Tim had come from a large loving family and I did not! We both saw the same situation and each of us developed a very different prognosis about what that meant for the future.

There is no such thing as objective reality and as such there is no truth only your truth. The lives we live are not so much about what happens but about what we make those things mean. In my marriage, my husband made the tragic events of my life mean that I was broken and as a result that also meant we shouldn't have kids. I didn't agree. Ultimately, I chose to leave that relationship to pursue my chance to meet someone who would see the potential in me. Someone, who like Dave, could appreciate that my tragedy had the potential to make me an even more loving mother, with valuable lessons and insights to pass on to my children.

Did you know ... ?

One of the principles of general semantics was the idea that reality is greatly influenced by the words we use to describe our experience. This is obvious if you consider that language is a fundamental instrument of communication, either with others or ourselves. Language was the only thing that turned a happy little lecture hall snack into a disgusting experience. Studies of indigenous cultures have shown that very often they don't have words to describe certain concepts and as a result, those things don't exist. For example, some Native American languages have no word for 'lie'.

There are about 200,000 words in common use in the English language. If you counted the words in the Oxford English Dictionary there are about 615,000. If you added scientific and technical words there would be millions of words to choose from. And yet it's estimated that the average person's working vocabulary is between 2,000 and 10,000 words. Many of those that have made the greatest contribution to the world have had a much wider grasp of language. William Shakespeare, for example, used 24,000 words in his writings and he coined hundreds more – such as amazement, perplex and majestic.

There is a story about twin boys who grew up together. Their father was in and out of prison and their lives were not easy. One of the twins became a successful lawyer and lived a productive life. The other twin spent many years in prison. They were interviewed and when asked separately why they ended up where they did, considering their background, each replied, 'I had no choice'. Both lived the same reality and yet each interpreted that reality differently. One assumed that because his father was a criminal then he had no choice but to follow in his fathers' footsteps. The other twin saw it very differently. To him he had no choice but to break the cycle because he knew that a life of crime was no way to live, he saw how it damaged his family and he was determined NOT to follow in his father's footsteps.

What made the difference? They experienced the same life as children, they even had the same genetic make-up, but their interpretation of those experiences differed. As a result their lives were very different. As

Frederick Langbridge said, *'Two men look out the same prison bars; one sees mud and the other stars'.*

Who writes history? Considering that the losers of most battles are either dead or imprisoned it's pretty safe to say that the winners write history. On that basis it can't possibly be an objective account. If we were able to go back and ask the losers of history for their versions, we would be reminded that the map is not the territory – there are always at least two sides to every story. And our history is no less concrete. It is merely a memory or representation of what we assumed happened at a moment in time. It is a captured assumption. If we can review those assumptions with new insights or new knowledge then we can change the past and release the hold that memories have over us. Old wounds and traumas will cease to exercise power over us and we can be free to move on.

You can change the past – the past is just one perspective of what happened. Understanding that there may be a myriad of other perspectives, all equally 'true' can release us from their grip. Korzybski was not the only great mind to arrive at the conclusion that objective reality doesn't exist. Carl Jung is known to have believed the same thing. He is quoted as saying, *'Perception is Projection'*, meaning that what we see outside us is merely a projection of what's inside us. Author and Booker Prize winner, Penelope Fitzgerald, said, *'no two people see the external world in exactly the same way. To every separate person a thing is what he thinks it is – in other words, not a thing, but a think'.*

Once you understand that truth and reality are nothing more than a composite of our beliefs and interpretations you have much more control over how you view the world. Outside events and influences cease to have the same power. No one can make you feel anything you don't want to feel. Whether you see everything as a setback and confirmation of your inadequacy, or whether you see it as a validation that you can overcome anything, is entirely up to you.

How to incorporate this wisdom into your life

Our internal maps of reality can change over time. What we consider possible, normal or sensible can evolve through a variety of ways:

- The people we meet
- The knowledge we gather
- The places we visit

Essentially our viewpoint changes when we expand our knowledge. We may meet someone from a different culture who gives us a completely new perspective. The same can be said about the places we visit, the programs we watch on TV or the books we read. While an afternoon of Jerry Springer isn't going to help in any way, every belief you have could be convincingly overturned by a visit to your local library. Ideas and knowledge contained in books, documentaries and on the Internet can open up your perspectives and give your life new meaning. And because these are so accessible, the possibilities for change are open to everyone.

If you want to be rich, for example, you must understand the landscape of wealth. You must understand the terminology and language of money. If you want to be a successful business owner, you have to expand your understanding of business so you can converse in that world.

Every time you read or hear a word you don't understand go and look it up in a good dictionary. Your task is to then use that word in conversation within the next 24 hours. If you expand your understanding, knowledge and vocabulary, you will expand your maps of reality and that in turn will expand the possibilities for your life.

Chapter 3

To the man who only has a hammer, everything he encounters begins to look like a nail. ~ Abraham H Maslow

Abraham Maslow was an American psychologist. His most famous work was the hierarchy of human needs, which we discuss in chapter 15. He is considered the father of humanistic psychology. Unlike his contemporaries, his work didn't focus on the abnormal or ill, instead he believed that everyone had the resources for growth and healing and that therapy's main aim was to help individuals to remove obstacles that would allow them to tap into that innate healing ability. This humanistic approach is, of course, the foundation of much of the therapy available today.

Maslow's quote is a reminder that our experience of the world depends on the tools we have at our disposal. If objective reality doesn't exist then what influences our interpretation?

One of the crucial pieces of the puzzle is our belief system. Our beliefs about what is true, right, real or possible are largely assembled in childhood through a process called conditioning. Essentially children learn what is 'normal' from the people around them. They will naturally pick up their ideas, perceptions, beliefs, attitudes of their primary caregivers. These beliefs about the world can have a massive impact on how your life turns out. If your parents were supportive and loving, encouraged you to pursue your dreams and taught you that anything was possible, then that is what you will believe to be true. If your parents did not believe those things and were jaded and disappointed by the results in their own lives, then chances are you will have adopted their limiting beliefs.

Einstein referred to limiting beliefs as the *'boundary conditions of our thinking'*. These ideas, concepts and opinions act as a box that we unconsciously put ourselves in from a very young age. What we consider possible is influenced by these rigid ideas – it is these ideas that make up the 'map' we referred to in the previous chapter. That is why it has often been said that the thinking that got us to where we are now will never get us to where we want to be.

Based on my experiences from early childhood, I developed a strong belief that life was meant to be hard. Much of my young life was characterised by constant struggle. I was always juggling multiple commitments and it felt like every second of my life had to have a 'purpose'. The idea of hard work was so deeply embedded in me; I just thought it was normal. The harder I worked to achieve something, the better I felt about it.

Even as a very young girl, I was addicted to the adrenalin rush and the satisfaction of achieving something that appeared difficult or challenging. By the age of six, my parents had me enrolled in private figure skating lessons, piano and ballet. As time went on, most days I was up at 5 am and on the ice for lessons by 6 am. My evenings and weekends were occupied with more skating lessons, ballet classes, piano practice and homework. It was a non-stop whirlwind of activities. The entire family joined in on my pursuits – my father became a skating judge, my mother designed and produced all of my costumes and my brother was dragged along to watch.

From the age of six, my life became incredibly serious. Even though I loved these pursuits and participating in them taught me numerous valuable lessons that I have employed in other areas of my life, the extreme nature of it all conditioned me to believe that I had to be flat out at all times just to be good enough. No matter what I did or what I achieved, it never seemed to be enough. My parents expected me to excel at whatever I did – the more I achieved, the more they expected. It got to the point that I would only receive feedback when I *didn't* achieve straight As or didn't perform well in the skating competition. I can remember at the age of 10 being absolutely terrified to drive home in the car with my father from a skating competition because he was upset that I didn't perform up to his expectations. He was incredibly vocal about my shortcomings and I felt ashamed when my peers would overhear him berating me in the corridor. I began to dislike going to the skating rink because I had already developed severe anxiety around my ability to perform to his standards.

I carried this addiction to achievement into adulthood. I am quite sure that I went to law school and obtained my chartered accounting designation, partly to please my parents and partly because it was something that required a lot of hard work and dedication. I never really stopped to ask myself what I truly wanted in life and what was important to *me*. I simply thought that if I worked hard enough, somehow, it would all work out in the end and I would be rewarded for my efforts. But the end never came – I never arrived at the 'destination' – in fact, as soon as my train pulled into the station of my last goal, I already had myself booked for the next journey up a steep and treacherous mountain. There was no time to remove my baggage from the train, no time for celebration and no pause for reflection on what I had already achieved. Even when things were easy or going well I looked for ways to make them difficult because hard work was familiar and comfortable.

Now, I'm not saying that a hard work ethic is a bad thing, as conditioned responses go it can be quite helpful. However, my unchallenged acceptance that life was meant to be hard was slowly killing me. The map I had in my mind of the way that life needed to be in order for me to be 'doing it properly' was holding me back from having what I truly wanted – love, happiness, fun, a sense of peace and enjoyment. My obsession with hard work was my hammer!

I recently did some time line therapy to release the limiting belief that everything in life had to be a struggle. I adopted a new belief that I can do anything and that everything comes easily for me. This represented a huge milestone because it allowed me to move beyond my limiting belief and write this book. In changing my mindset about the project, I was able to break the book down into easy chunks that I could tackle quickly and easily without it turning into a chore.

Limiting beliefs are so important because they influence what we consider to be 'normal' and 'possible'. There are plenty of examples of limiting beliefs in history. For years people thought the world was flat. And that belief stopped people from exploring the world because they thought if they went too far, they would fall off the edge! Luckily, or unluckily depending on who you ask, Columbus didn't think it was true and set off to discover the new world.

It was widely thought that when Roger Bannister broke the four-minute mile there was a universal limiting belief that it simply could not be done. There was uncertainty around whether it would ever be broken. It stood as a milestone for many runners. Ironically, as soon as Bannister broke the barrier, a slew of people followed suit almost immediately. The artificial limit was finally broken and with it the uncertainty that had stopped so many from even trying. As a result, what had previously been seen as an unobtainable goal became obtainable and other runners soon followed.

In the 1950s kidney transplants were possible, but people were afraid to go under the knife – for obvious reasons. Then a doctor in Chicago conducted a successful transplant and published his results. Soon transplants became commonplace and have saved thousands of lives. Transplant patients believed that it was possible and that they could survive. As a result, success rates have soared.

If you go back just 100 years, the idea of sending a man to the moon would have been considered ludicrous and you'd have probably been locked up in an asylum for thinking it was possible, yet in 1969, Neil Armstrong became the first man to step onto the surface of the moon. In 1961 when John F Kennedy declared that America would put a man on the moon in less than a decade, he immediately woke up the scientific community. Prior to that statement, a lunar landing seemed an impossible dream, or at the very least, something that was a long way off. Kennedy's statement represented a new boundary condition in the collective mind of the nation. Interestingly, instead of focusing on why it couldn't be done, America's greatest scientific minds began directing their energies and attentions toward what needed to be done in order to achieve it.

The tricky part of limiting beliefs is that they are predominately unconscious. If you think of your mind as an iceberg, then the tip of the iceberg is your conscious mind. The larger, more substantial part of the iceberg represents your subconscious mind. As adults, we are simply not aware of the thinking that is limiting our experiences and results because it is below the surface in the subconscious mind. For example, a child who has grown up in poverty will have a very different concept about money than someone who has not experienced money worries or whose parents never discussed money troubles. A child brought up in poverty is likely to have heard all sorts of reasons and excuses about why they had no money. They've probably also heard about how all rich people are crooks and that money is the root of all evil and how being poor is therefore honourable.

The adult may not consciously remember these ideas but whenever they have a little money they find that it slips through their fingers very quickly. Even if they are promoted and promoted, they never seem to have enough money. Why? Because the unconscious limiting beliefs they have about money impacts their financial experience. It has been said, if you want to know what you were thinking yesterday about wealth, health, relationships etc, all you need to do is look at your results today. By making an effort to expand your thinking you will expand your toolkit for life and ensure that you have far more choice in how you treat the events and situations that arise. That way you will be able to apply the appropriate tool to any given situation giving you the confidence to know that you can deal with whatever comes your way.

Did you know ... ?

No doubt you'll have heard of Pavlov's dogs. Pavlov conditioned his dogs to salivate at the sound of a bell even when there was no food present. You're probably wondering what that has to do with your reality ...

The tools we use in life or the maps we use to navigate life are all created through the exact same process – conditioned response. Pavlov fed his dogs and the dogs salivated. He then fed his dogs while ringing a bell and the dogs still salivated. Eventually he only had to ring the bell and the dogs salivated.

Pavlov's discovery led to significant developments in comparative psychology. As children growing up, we learn from the people and environment around us. In order to make sense of the information we make assumptions and associations that are not always accurate or helpful. Say as a small child you run to the shops to buy some milk for your mum and on the way home a dog jumps up at a garden gate and barks and you get such a shock you drop the milk bottle and cut your finger. Because this is an emotional experience your brain looks for the common characteristics of the event so it can log it in the memory banks of 'things to avoid'. Your child's mind unconsciously comes up with milk = broken glass = dog = pain. Over time that may be further simplified to dog = pain. As an adult you get very uncomfortable around dogs and have no idea why because the conscious memory of the incident is long gone. But it was so emotionally charged for you that you immediately create a conditioned response. From that point forward, if any one or more of those stimuli are present you slip unconsciously into autopilot and feel the same anxiety and shock you did as a child.

In a lifetime you have probably created thousands of these conditioned responses or default settings that influence your life. Very often they are harmless and make little difference to you on a daily basis but if the conditioned response is strong enough it can have a profound effect. It becomes your hammer that makes everything look like a nail.

The brain has a pre-disposition to use and re-use our automatic responses because it's quicker – even when the response doesn't fit the situation. It's a knee-jerk reaction based on some long forgotten assumption. From time to time, these responses need to be changed or adjusted to produce the results that we say we want in our lives at a conscious level.

How to incorporate this wisdom into your life

Have you ever had the experience where something happened and you had an immediate emotional reaction? Then when the dust settled you couldn't quite believe how much you over reacted?

Thinking about that episode can you think of another similar situation where this has happened? Take some time and write down every example you can remember where you have been confused about the intensity of your reaction. Taking each situation in turn, write down as much detail as possible. Pay particular attention to who was involved, location, what was said and how you felt. Are there any similarities between the events? Being able to see the connection between the events can go a long way in changing the behaviour or learning to anticipate it.

Chapter 4

What I focus on in life is what I get. ~ W Mitchell

W Mitchell is an inspiration to anyone who knows his story. He is a successful businessman and was also involved in politics but what he's known for most is his unwavering courage and indomitable human spirit in the face of life-changing challenges. First, he had a motorcycle accident that burned 65% of his body. He recovered from that ordeal, albeit permanently scarred, and went on to suffer an airplane crash that took away his ability to walk. None of this dented his ability to live with grace, good humour and passion.

What we focus on plays a huge part in the reality we experience. So far we've talked about limiting beliefs and maps of reality that influence our experience. In other words what we experience is much more dependent on what happens on the inside than on the outside. What happens in our mind is much more relevant than what actually happens in life!

At any one time during your waking experience, it is estimated that your nervous system is bombarded by over 2 million bits of sensory data per second about events happening around you. You receive and process this information via your five senses – sight, sound, touch, smell and taste. What science has found, however, is that your mind is incredibly selective about what information it pays attention to because it cannot hope to process all of it? It unconsciously filters out the information that is not relevant at the time. These relevance filters essentially delete, distort or generalise the information according to your model of the world. At the end of this unconscious filtering process, you are left with your perception of the world and this perception is based on roughly 134 bits (or 7 +/- 2 chunks) of information.

So of the possible 2 million bits of information that we could interpret at any one time we are actually only aware of a tiny fraction. Our interpretation of what's happening around us is based on less than 1% of what's actually going on!

The reason for this is simple. If we were consciously aware of all the information that is potentially available to us at any given moment – we'd go crazy. So the brain helps by applying filters based on past experiences, events, situations, conditioned responses, thoughts and feelings to determine what is important.

These filters therefore affect what we focus on in life and ultimately affect our experience. If we are filtering for love, abundance, family and contribution, the world that we experience will be drastically different than the one where the observer is filtering for poverty, hatred, isolation and depression.

You probably experienced this in your own life. Think of a time when you made an important decision – it might have been to start a family, marry your sweetheart, purchase a brand new car or travel to an exotic destination. No matter what that decision was, just allow your mind to go back to that time now and remember the process that you went through in reaching that critical decision. You may remember that once you began focusing your attention on the decision, you actually became more aware of it in your immediate environment.

For those of you who had your eye on a little red sports car, perhaps you began to notice all the other little red sports cars on the road. Or maybe you were thinking of having a baby and suddenly began to see pregnant women or women with infants in prams everywhere you went? It appears that little red sports cars and pregnant women suddenly multiplied overnight. They didn't, they were always there; you just didn't notice them before because they were not included in the 134 bits of information per second you became conscious of.

Up until the age of six, my parents and I lived in the basement of my maternal grandparent's home in a very small town in Alberta, Canada. My grandmother, Alvina Kutinsky, took care of me during the day while my parents were at work. I look back on those times as some of the happiest that I have ever had. I was my grandmother's shadow – baking pies with her in the kitchen, pulling weeds out of the flowerbeds and sitting on my little white chair in the backyard eating baby vegetables that she pulled out of her garden and cleaned with the hose on the side of the house. Her loving approval, ever-watchful eye and unending patience had a profound effect on me.

We were inseparable. Under her care and tutelage, I learned by the age of five how to read and write, count money and I could sing all of the Christmas carols and various other children's songs in both English and German. This was a distinct advantage to me because I commenced Grade 1 with an enormous sense of confidence and enthusiasm – and I carried that with me throughout my school years and on into university.

My grandmother never learned how to drive a car so we spent most of our days together at or very near to the house. Around the age of three, my grandmother decided that it might be a nice idea for us to take the bus downtown and do a little bit of shopping. Prior to leaving the house she sat me down to have a little chat about eating the right foods. My grandmother was pretty particular about teaching me to eat healthy foods. She made everything from scratch and always insisted that I have a healthy breakfast and frequent balanced meals throughout the day. Her refrigerator was always packed with lots of interesting, natural foods. I, however, was not too keen on green vegetables and I had already begun to develop a sweet tooth.

She explained to me very clearly that day that if I didn't start watching what I ate, I was going to put on a lot of weight and become very fat. I listened very intently and was impacted by what she said.

We caught the bus to the city across the street from her home. I can still remember feeling very grown up and excited about the impending adventure. Shortly after we sat down, I began looking around at all of the other passengers. To be fair, I had led a pretty sheltered life and everyone and everything seemed very new and interesting. It wasn't long before I spotted a lady a couple of rows back that was extremely overweight. To the horror of my grandmother, I jumped up on my seat, pointed directly at the woman and yelled 'Grandma, grandma, look … that lady has been eating way too many candies and she has gotten herself fat! Grandma, please tell her to stop eating all the candies!'

The look on my grandmother's face was priceless. She reached up quietly and pulled the bell without saying a word, we got off as soon as possible. We walked about eight blocks home that day and my grandmother explained to me in great detail how people come in all shapes, sizes, colours etc. She was absolutely mortified at my outburst. It was an excellent example of how when you focus on something, it brings it to the forefront of your conscious attention and it affects how you experience the world.

About three weeks later my grandmother thought it might be safe for us to attempt to take the bus again – this time we were going into the city to see the circus. I had never been to a circus but I had some idea of what to expect because it had been advertised on the TV and I had read about it in my books. To say I was excited would have been a huge understatement; I was absolutely beside myself with anticipation.

Before getting on the bus, grandma reminded me about the fact that people came in all shapes, sizes and colours and that it wasn't nice to point at people. We again boarded the bus and found ourselves a nice bench seat right in the middle. As children do, I began to look around examining the other passengers and watching the houses and street signs go by. Out of the corner of my eye, I caught a glimpse of a woman – a woman wearing an incredible amount of makeup. With all the innocence of a young child and the anticipation of my first real circus, I popped up in my seat and exclaimed 'Grandma grandma, look at the CLOWN!'

My grandmother attempted to quiet me down but there was just no stopping me. Everyone, including the lady I was pointing at, began to laugh and my grandmother quietly reached up without saying a word, pulled the string to get the bus to stop and we got off at the next stop. Even though she was incredibly embarrassed, I distinctly remember that she never raised her voice or reprimanded me … during our long walk home she just quietly gave me my first lesson at the age of three on why women wear cosmetics. And come to think of it, I don't believe that I actually ever rode the bus again until many years later when we moved to another suburb and I needed to board a school bus to attend junior high school.

Many years later I remember attending a book launch for a book written by two Canadian mountaineers, Jamie Clarke and Alan Hobson. The

Did you know ... ?

Harvard ran some experiments in 2004 that illustrated just how blind we can be when it comes to the world around us. They asked a group of people to watch a video of a game of basketball and count how many passes were made on one particular team.

A simple task that would require a little concentration but nothing more strenuous! During the video someone in a gorilla suit walked onto the court and wandered through the players for a full seven seconds. At one point the gorilla even turned to the camera and beat its chest! When asked about their experience of watching the video less than half the viewers mentioned the gorilla! Some of the students were so focused on counting the passes of the players that they failed to notice a gorilla in their midst! How is that possible? Because we are only ever translating a fraction of the potential information available to us and what we see is very much dependent on what we are focused on.

book was about their attempts and eventual success in climbing Mount Everest. The Power of Passion is far more than a simple mountaineering tale: it is a story about real life – the pursuit of dreams, the importance of teamwork and courage, the precarious balance between tenacity and tragedy and the triumph of the human spirit.

During the presentation in Calgary, Jamie showed video footage of parts of the climb – there were times when he and the others on the expedition were walking across what seemed like a bottom-less crevices on rickety metal ladders with 40lbs of gear on their backs. It was one of the most dangerous and terrifying adventures I have ever seen.

After the presentation, someone in the crowd stood up and asked him, 'Didn't you ever look down and think, my God, if I fall now, I will surely die.' I will never forget Jamie's response. He said, 'That would be your first and last mistake – you should never look down. If there is one thing I have learned in climbing and in life, it is this, wherever you look or focus your attention that is EXACTLY where you are going to end up. If you look up to the top of your own personal Everest or down the crevice, it is not only scary but also incredibly dangerous. That is why I focused 100% of my attention on where I was at and just three steps ahead.'

This concept is also taught in advanced driving. If your car goes into a skid you must focus on where you want to go – not the wall or obstacle in front of you. The quickest way to crash is to take your eye off where you want to go and instead focus on your problems! So make sure you focus on where it is you want to go not where you don't want to go – and you'll be astonished at just how far you *can* go!

How to incorporate this wisdom into your life

If your experience of life is affected by what you are focusing on it follows that if you change your focus you will change your life. Think about it? What ARE you filtering for every single day? Do creative ideas and money flow quickly and easily to you or are you focused on the things you don't want – like mounting bills?

Write down the top five things that have been occupying your mind lately. Is your focus on what you want or is your focus geared more heavily toward what you don't want? Remember we get what we focus on, so if you're not getting the results you want, NOW would be a good time to shift your focus.

Chapter 5

The real voyage of discovery consists not in seeking new landscapes but in having new eyes. ~ Marcel Proust

Marcel Proust (1871-1922) was a French novelist, essayist and critic, best known as the author of *In Search of Lost Time*, a monumental work of 20th century fiction dealing with the decline of the aristocracy and the consequent rise of the middle class.

When we think of changing aspects of our lives, we generally imagine making physical changes. That may be moving house, moving jobs or even moving countries. And certainly those types of change can be refreshing and valuable in breaking patterns and making a fresh start. But the interesting thing about a fresh start is that they never stay that fresh for long. The irritating part of physical change is that you often stay the same – wherever you go, there you are. As time passes you are forced to realise that while there may be a new job with new colleagues or a new view out the window of your kitchen – you are exactly the same!

This quote reminds me that real change doesn't require removalists and packing boxes. It doesn't require updated resumes or impeccable references and it certainly doesn't need a passport – what it needs is courage to see your life with new eyes.

I was reminded of this once again when I recently had coffee with two girlfriends. At the time all three of us had recently been made redundant from our jobs. One of my friends suspected that the redundancy program was a convenient way for her employer to legitimately get rid of her so that the company did not have to pay for her maternity leave. Nicole had been with the company, a well-known sporting organisation, for four years and had poured her heart and soul into the position. Ironically, although the redundancy was questionable from an ethical and legal perspective, she didn't see it as the end of the world. Even though she and her partner really had their hands full – they were in the middle of house renovations, huge financial commitments, a relocation and they had their first child on the way. Nonetheless, she seemed steadfastly focused on her health, family and the possibility of starting her own consulting business.

I remember being in awe of her positive outlook. My other friend was clearly more outraged and apprehensive about the uncertainty redundancy brought all of us. Her discomfort was palpable and her fear and anger were rising as the conversation progressed. Financial security and loyalty were incredibly important values to her and this incident seemed to fly in the face of everything that she held dear. Even when the conversation naturally moved onto new topics, this friend would find a way to draw us all back into a discussion about the injustice of our situations.

One of the things that really struck me was that the event itself (the redundancy) was neither good nor bad, right nor wrong. Each of us had vastly different values and views about the necessity, challenge or excitement of having a job and the fear, freedom or new possibilities associated with redundancy. If the event was the same and yet we each viewed it through different eyes, what made the difference?

It came down to the values that we had about particular aspects of our lives. It was quite clear that our experience of the world occurred internally not externally. And that made me wonder ... Was it possible to change things internally to increase the joy and fulfilment that we experience in life so that we don't find ourselves constantly at the mercy of unpredictable changes in our environment? And the answer almost certainly is 'yes'.
Our core values create our unique model or perception of the world. Values are essentially the way in which we judge good and bad, right and wrong, normal and abnormal.

One of my friends viewed the redundancy as unjust and unfair and that hurt her values. The other may also have felt her redundancy was unfair but she valued other things more highly. She was able to see it as a new adventure and an opportunity to kick start her own business.

Sociologist Morris Massey identified the three major periods in our lives where we develop and consolidate our values. During the Imprint Period (from birth to seven), we are like sponges, absorbing everything and accepting much of it as true – especially if it comes from a parent or authority figure. A child will develop their sense of right and wrong, good and bad in this deeply impressionable period. The values learned during this period will be very deeply imprinted and are the most difficult to change in later life. Often we have no conscious memory of the values learned during this period and therefore we accept them as 'truths' and do not question them.

Between eight and 13, we copy others (our parents, relatives, teachers, superhero's, celebrities etc) and this is known as the Modelling Period. Instead of blind acceptance we try on various values, like different pieces of clothing, to see how they feel. Individuals looked up to and seen as knowledgeable will particularly influence children during this period. The Socialization period (13 to 21) is largely characterised by the influence of peers, media and the Internet. During this period, we are often looking to break free from our earlier, authority based socialisation and to turn to role models our own age who naturally seem more like us.

According to Massey, 90 per cent of our values are formed and integrated by age 10 and 100 per cent by age 20. In his book, Massey asks *Where were you when you were ten?'* What was going on around you at that formative time that crystallised the values and beliefs that you have carried forward until today? Those who grew up in the Great Depression place a different value and emphasis on money and credit than children who were born in economically prosperous times, for example. These values rarely change (if at all) unless there is a Significant Emotional Event (SEE) or if there is a deliberate or artificial creation of an SEE in which a specific value is identified, targeted and shifted. The SEE allows you to re-assess your values because you suddenly see the world in a completely different light.

Essentially, values are the things that are important to us and they exert a powerful influence on our lives. Values determine how we relate to others, how we perform at our jobs, what products we purchase, how much money we earn, our religious convictions, leisure pastimes we pursue, who we vote for etc. Your life is a reflection, albeit an unconscious reflection, of what you value.

On the surface we all have reasons for doing what we do and to us it all makes perfect sense. However, lurking beneath the surface is an entirely different set of reasons that are much more powerful and more difficult to articulate. These reasons – our values – constitute the sum total of our experiences to date.

Did you know ... ?

There are two main categories of values – towards values and away-from values. Unsurprisingly one represents values that you are moving toward and want to experience and the other represents values that you are trying to avoid or move away from. Away-from motivation is less reliable than towards because it creates inconsistent results. For example, if you are motivated not to be overweight you will diet for a while until you lose the weight and then the motivation will subside because you are no longer driven 'not to be fat'. You take your eye off the ball and three months later you realise that you are overweight again and you have to start the process again. The same could be said if you were driven 'not to be poor'. You might work hard in your business and make lots of money. Once you are 'not poor', you will relax, the business will take a backward step and you will lose money – and so the process must start again. If on the other hand, you value 'being rich' which is a positive toward value, you wouldn't have the inconsistency of results. The same if you valued being slim, fit and healthy.

If there is an area of your life where you are not achieving, there might be a lot of away-from motivation. I remember seeing Oprah Winfrey interviewed about motivation on Larry King. She asked him to clarify if he meant her motivation for 'working' or 'working out'. She admitted that, 'my motivation to work is easy – I want to create understanding, abundance, love, compassion and accountability. On the topic of working out, that is also easy, I don't want to have a fat butt.' Looking at Oprah's results is easy to see that toward values have much more power. For years she struggled with her fluctuating weight and when you consider the relative motivational force between toward and away from values, it's easy to see why!

Human nature is actually very transparent. We simply will not spend time on something that is not important (or of value) to us. So for example, an overweight person may say that they value their health and are really committed to getting in shape but if they remain overweight, then the evidence about their hierarchy of values in relation to their life is obvious for all to see.

It may very well be true that they do value their health but it's obvious from their results, that they value something else more. Perhaps they value freedom, comfort or spontaneity more than health? Being able to enjoy the food they love whenever they want is more important to them than physical wellbeing. Perhaps food represents connection and love and that is more important than health. John W Gardner summed it up so clearly when he said, '*All of us celebrate our values in our behaviour*'.

This is what is referred to as a values conflict. If you have ever had the experience of wanting to do something consciously and yet no matter how much you try or want to change nothing really transpires, you have experienced this phenomenon. Or if you do force through change by will power alone, the alteration this phenomenon you have experienced first hand is short lived. The reason for this could come down to a values conflict. What you say you want directly contradicts what you unconsciously value. Or what you say you want is contradicted by another value that holds more power for you.

Not everyone's value system supports them in achieving their goals and dreams. Let's take the example of money – we all need to make money in order to live but each of us has a uniquely different way of viewing it in the context of our lives. Most people would like to have more money, and for some it becomes an obsession, but if you scratch the surface of that conscious desire you will find all manner of opinions or ideas about money that make it virtually impossible to meet your conscious dreams. If, for example, you value honesty and integrity and you secretly harbour a conviction that people with money are dishonest and must have sold their soul to obtain vast wealth – do you honestly think your subconscious mind is going to harness its awesome power to make you rich?

The conscious mind is a puny weakling compared to the might of the subconscious mind. Your values reside in your subconscious mind and unless they are congruently aligned to your conscious desires and dreams you won't achieve what it is you are seeking.

And yet if you can uncover your values and find out the rules that govern them you have the opportunity to apply those insights to your life so that you can see any landscape through new eyes.

As human beings we are a result of our yesterdays. We are the living expression of our unconscious drivers. Values are like our 'eyes' – how we see and judge the world and events as right and wrong, good and bad, normal and abnormal. They help us create our model of the world and our results. Once we become conscious of what they are in different aspects of our lives, we can change them in order to support and drive us towards our goals and dreams.

You can adjust the jobs, homes or people in your life a thousand times but wherever you go, there you will be. But if you change your eyes, the way that you see and look at the world, you can create an entirely new world without ever having to pack a single box or say a single goodbye.

We may not always have the ability to physically leave the landscape we find ourselves in but we always have the ability to change what we see by virtue of adjusting what we focus our eyes and our mind on.

How to incorporate this wisdom into your life

By becoming conscious of your values in a particular aspect of your life and whether they empower or impede you in the attainment of your goals, you can take the first step toward manifesting what you say that you really want.

STEP 1: Chose an area of your life that you'd like to improve:

- Career/work/school
- Relationships – social, intimate
- Family
- Health/fitness
- Personal growth
- Spirituality
- Other

STEP 2: Ask yourself *'What is important to me in or about* (insert topic here – eg, my career)*?'* Begin to list each of the words or short phrases that come to mind. It is not important at this stage to concern yourself with priorities or preferences, just list as many as you can think of. Ideally, try to come up with a list of about 15 to 25 values.

AREA OF FOCUS _____

VALUES:

_____	_____
_____	_____
_____	_____
_____	_____
_____	_____
_____	_____
_____	_____

STEP 3: Before we can make changes, we need to identify the priorities of the various values in this aspect of your life TODAY. Go back to Step 2 and begin numbering each value. *Place a number (1 being most important, 2 next most important) to the LEFT of each value based on the RESULTS that you have TODAY in this aspect of your life.* Remember, if you want to know what you were really thinking about finances or your relationships, you need only look at your bank account or the quality of your relationships today. It is important to be honest with yourself – this step is the key to helping you uncover where the incongruency lies between your current values and what you really want (your goals).

STEP 4: *Now, on the right hand side of each value above, rank each in the order of how you would like them to be in this area of your life (1 being most important, 2 next most important).* If you are having difficulty determining what the optimal ranking should be, think of someone who you know or have heard of that is very successful in this area – what would this person value as most important? For example, if you have chosen finance as you area of focus and you are unsure which values should be your highest priorities; imagine how someone like Richard Branson or Donald Trump would rank the values.

STEP 5: You may have already begun to notice and identify several key learnings and insights that you would like to focus on as a result of completing your list and rankings. Values are far more powerful and influential than most of us realise. They drive our decisions, formulate our self-worth and ultimately affect our RESULTS. Actions always speak louder than words so look at your results. What you say that you want is one thing. What you do about it is another. Values always show up in a person's actions.

Select one value from your list above that you want to concentrate on today – perhaps you have identified knowledge/learning as a key value in the context of finances, yet your current ranking (based on your results) is very low. Close your eyes and create an image in your mind of what knowledge/learning looks like – what do you see, what do you hear, how do you feel, what do people say around you, what are you saying to yourself about knowledge/learning? Make that mental picture extremely vibrant and compelling to you. Now ask yourself 'What three actions can I take immediately in order to demonstrate my new commitment to this value in my life?' Open your eyes and write three actions down plus assign a date (within three days of today) when they will be completed. Share your learnings and the three action steps with a friend and ask them to help keep you accountable to yourself regarding the deadlines. The steps do not need to be huge. The important key is to identify three steps and take action immediately. For example, if your value is knowledge/learning, you could:

(1) Select a role model like Donald Trump and purchase a book on how he built his empire;
(2) Make some calls to interview a professional advisor who can help get your finances organised; and
(3) Make a detailed inventory of your current financial situation and key goals for the future.

ACTIONS   COMPLETED BY

_____   _____
_____   _____
_____   _____
_____   _____

Chapter 6

If you want a quality, act as if you already had it. Try the 'as if' technique. ~ William James

William James was a pioneering American psychologist and philosopher. One of his best-known philosophical ideas is that of pragmatism – the value of a truth depends upon its use to the person who holds it. Although he died in 1910, his influence is still felt today in the field of psychology. He in turn was influenced by many of his own giants including his godfather Ralph Waldo Emerson.

Science has proven that the brain does not know the difference between what is vividly imagined and reality. If we experience only a fraction of what is possible in terms of the stimuli that we notice or pay attention to, and our experiences are directly influenced by what we value, believe and expect, then it follows that by changing what is happening in our mind we can actually change our entire reality.

I remember when I first heard about this concept. My ex-sister in law, Harwant, had been to an interview one day and we were catching up for coffee so that she could tell me about it. She said that the interviewer had asked her what her motto for life was. Harwant is a very energetic, free-spirited woman so she replied – *'fake it until you make it'*. At the time that I heard this, I was absolutely mortified. Surely this is something that one may think but would never actually say out loud, especially in an interview? I thought she was mad. In my mind, she had blown any chance of getting the job with that statement.

However, I was wrong to jump to this premature conclusion and in time I began to appreciate the wisdom in what she said. It was not at all about pretending to be someone that you are not – like pretending to be an artist when you are a builder or telling people that you've won the lottery in the hope that it will come about. That's lying and just plain counterproductive! Acting 'as if' or 'faking it until you make it' is about adopting the characteristics and personality traits of someone you admire or who has already achieved the goal that you aspire to. In the formula BE x DO = HAVE, it is about becoming the type of person you aspire to be and taking actions relevant to that objective that will result in you experiencing that goal in life.

Did you know ... ?

If you are scared of spiders your body will have the exact same physiological reaction whether you think of a spider, see a spider or simply hear the word 'spider'. The external result is exactly the same regardless of whether the spider exists or not. Said another way, whether there is a poisonous spider on your shoulder or whether you only believe that there is, your physical reaction will be the same.

In the same way, if you act as if you are confident, your brain chemistry behaves in exactly the same way as if you really are confident. There is no biological or chemical difference in the body between something imagined, remembered or experienced.

One of the wonderful things about personal characteristics or emotional states is that if you pretend to have them, then you have them immediately. If you act as though you are courageous, then you will be courageous. If you act as though you are confident and take on the persona of someone who is confident, then you become confident. Since the mind doesn't know the difference between a real or imagined event, then acting 'as if' is a logical and sensible solution to temporary uncertainty!

If you act as if you are happy you may be amazed to realise that you are. Because our mind has such a profound influence on our external experience, adopting and making beneficial emotional states a regular habit is the first step to truly mastering your life. These characteristics or personal attributes are emotional states, not future outcomes or goals, and as such they can be achieved immediately. As Henry David Thoreau so rightly points out, *'I do not know how to distinguish between our waking life and a dream. Are we not always living the life that we imagine we are?'* All that we are and have experienced to date is a result of what we have imagined to be true in our minds. If we are unhappy with the results, our experience can be changed as quickly as we can change our minds and imagine a new meaning.

It is a bit like role-playing. We all have certain roles that we play in our lives. They may be wife, mother, co-worker, friend or student. Each role has unwritten and unspecified parameters – set by you and often by society's expectations of those roles.

The great thing about the concept of roles is they can be used to your advantage if you know how. They act as an invisible costume that we slip in and out of depending on what is required of us. Some of us have very well developed role of 'victim', for example. Or perhaps we slip easily into the role of 'caregiver' or 'fighter'. These roles also influence how we engage with the world around us. Zig Ziglar summed it up eloquently when he said, *'you cannot climb the ladder of success dressed in the costume of failure'.*

As Shakespeare said in his play As You Like It, *'All the world's a stage. And all the men and women merely players. They have their exits and their entrances, and one man in his time plays many parts'.* We each have the choice each day as to which part we will play and which costume we will wear. Many of us play the same role every day without stopping to question why? Those roles can be neither inspiring nor exciting and yet we accept them as a fait accompli. In many ways it reminds me of the little child who is relegated to the supporting role of 'tree' or 'flower' in the primary school play. We all know the one – he stands in the corner with the ridiculous costume on but is never given the chance to speak or sing with the others. That child is on stage with the rest of the class but never really has the chance to shine or take centre stage – to play the lead character and command the attention and applause of an adoring audience.

Eventually that child grows up but has become so accustomed to playing the supporting role that he does not realise the limitless possibilities available to him – successful entrepreneur, loving father, skilful public speaker, leader in the community etc. He is 30 years old and still getting up each and every day to put on his 'tree' costume and stand on the sidelines of his own life. The school play is long over yet he is still living the life he imagined in his head when he was a little boy.

Fortunately, it's never too late to create some new empowering roles for yourself that allow you to slip on the mental costume of courage, determination, unbridled enthusiasm or whatever personality trait or emotional state that you most want to incorporate into your life. In my own life I use this technique almost every single day – especially when I am called upon to speak to large groups of people. In many respects I am a naturally introverted person. In order to ensure that I deliver my message and connect with my audience in an interesting and compelling way, I visualise myself taking on the persona of someone who has an abundance of passion, confidence, courage, energy, charisma, spontaneity and power.

For me, the person that I most aspire to be like and look up to is Anthony Robbins – he embodies the heartfelt compassion, excitement, professionalism and commitment to excellence that typifies the quintessential motivational speaker. I literally step into the shoes of this character that I have created around Tony in my own mind immediately before I go on stage and I become consumed and invigorated by those character traits. I have been doing it for so many years that it has become an automatic habit – I can feel my energy, my physiology and my personality changing as soon as my feet touch the stage. I literally become the person that I need to be in that moment in order to do what would normally be outside of my comfort zone – speaking in front of thousands of people. I have been doing it for so long that it has become a part of who I am now – I started out faking it and then I actually became the person that I imagined in my mind.

You see many years ago I made an important decision that changed my life – I decided that I would rather wear an outlandish pair of 'rose-coloured' glasses that support and empower me, than a 'realistic' set of prescription lenses that stopped me from truly seeing and living my dreams. Each and every day when we wake up, we all have the choice of which lenses, attire or uniform to put on. The choice has always been yours and the possibilities are infinite. Today is a brand new day – you can choose to embody characteristics and personality traits that empower you and move you closer to your goals or you can chose to adopt a persona of negativity and pessimism. Your mind doesn't know the difference between reality and what you vividly imagine so why not chose something that's going to make your life richer, happier and more fulfilling?

It's time to cast aside your 'tree' costume ... you won't need that anymore. You can be anything that you choose to imagine right now. Fake it until you make it! Trust me, it will be a short trip.

How to incorporate this wisdom into your life

Write down ten people that you admire and why you admire them. List all the specific traits and characteristics about that person that you would love to possess yourself.

Say you would love more self-confidence and you have written that you admire Oprah Winfrey because of her strong opinions and ability to influence others. Next time you are in a situation that requires self confidence take a moment to ask yourself, 'What would Oprah do right now?' Getting that shift in perspective can allow you to assume that costume of self-confidence and act as if you are already self-confident. Remember, the brain doesn't know the difference between a real or imagined experience – in other words if you *act as if*, you will embody that characteristic in real life.

You could also imagine and create a few roles that you could adopt (like a costume) when you need them. Just like a super hero's costume or magical cape, you could mentally assume the persona of 'Queen of Confidence' or 'Determinator'. Have fun with this and embrace your super hero persona whenever you need a little mental boost!

Chapter 7

Get out of your head, it's a bad neighbourhood! ~ Jeff Poule

> Jeff Poule was born and raised in Corner Brook, Newfoundland and has been practising law in the province of Alberta since 1981. He is one of the most decent men that I have ever had the privilege of knowing and one who takes his role, responsibility and solemn oath to serve and protect the public, very seriously. I became a client of his in 2000 and my life was forever changed, not so much by what he did as my attorney, but more by what he taught me about life and living.

I love this quote and I still laugh out loud every time I think of it or share it with someone who needs to hear it. Jeff became my lawyer in 2000 and helped me with various projects in relation to a business that I owned, From Here to Maternity (more on that in Chapter 11). He is incredibly good at what he does and I am forever grateful for his knowledge and assistance. Towards the end of his work with me in a corporate capacity, he also became my divorce lawyer and confidant. He and his wife invited me over to their home many times and I was always amazed at his optimistic perspective on life and his ability to balance his work and personal life.

September 11, 2001 was a day that no one will forget. In addition to the tragedy, horror and aftermath of the terrorist attacks, my marriage began to unravel and I witnessed the collapse of the business I had sunk my whole heart and life savings into. I felt overwhelmed by emotions in the months that followed and I was very fearful about my ability to make it on my own and to re-build my life.

One day in October, while sitting in Jeff's office going through piles of legal documents and dealing with a myriad of issues, I began to lament about the tragedy of my own personal situation and the doubts I had about being able to cope and recover. Jeff leaned toward me and said, in a matter of fact manner that only he could get away with 'Get out of your head Rhondalynn, it's a bad neighbourhood.'

I don't think any truer words have ever been spoken. Not only was I not mad about the fact that he was obviously giving me a hard time, I burst out laughing and realised in an instant that I could change my world simply by changing my mind and my thoughts.

The truth is we sometimes get so caught up in the mental cycles of negativity that we simply can't break out of it. We can't see any other perspective or any way out of the distress. It is like being trapped in a dark room without any windows or doors! No direction or options seem available and there is a sense of hopelessness.

Everyone has bad days and no amount of positive thinking or self-help information is going to change that. It's part of being human. There has to be downs otherwise you wouldn't appreciate the ups. Experiencing those highs and lows are just a normal part of life. Living full time in a bad emotional place, however, is not really living at all. It's existing - what sort of life is that? You have to be able to recognise the landscape you're in and do something about it. Just as there are affluent and poor neighbourhoods in every city there are good suburbs in your mind and those that resemble the ghetto. When you recognise that and can work out where you are at any given time, you can make sure you don't stop in the bad sections of town!

For me it took years of work and searching for answers. I desperately wanted to find the magic bullet that would suddenly make everything make sense. I wanted to be able to feel again, without it being so painful. But I can honestly say there is no magic bullet, no 'secret', apart from the amazing zone between your ears – your mind.

My lawyer made what could have been construed as a flippant, uncaring comment about my mental and emotional state, but I know it was said with care and, above all, humour. He wanted me to snap out of my hopelessness – even if only for a second. And I did. I was able to see for the first time that it wasn't always going to be so bad. And it was an important first step toward recovering my emotional equilibrium.

Nothing is permanent. Shifting our perception can radically alter everything – even things that appear to be fixed. Life is a cycle of seasons, with every ending there is always a renewal or a new beginning.

When Jeff told me to get out of my head, his terminology made me laugh. Humour is a brilliant way to break someone's pattern and improve his or her state of mind. The idea that humour might actually create a healing environment within the body is gaining respect among some scientists in a field called psychoneuroimmunology. This is the study of the connection and interaction between the brain and the disease-fighting immune system of the body.

But it's not a new idea. There is evidence going back at least as far as the ancient Greeks that entertainment could be beneficial to the healing process. The Greeks were known for building their hospitals next to amphitheaters so that the patients could benefit from the entertainment.

Did you know ... ?

Have you ever seen the film *Patch Adams*? Did you realise that Hunter 'Patch' Adams was a real person? He began medical school without an undergraduate degree, and earned his Doctor of Medicine degree in 1973 at the Medical College of Virginia, part of the Virginia Commonwealth University. During his studies he was troubled by the traditional 'men in white coats' medicine that treated illnesses and not people and often showed patients' very little compassion – doctors would talk about their patients as though they were not there and remained emotionally distant from the patient and their healing process.

Patch felt this was a mistake and along with some fellow medical students set up the Gesundheit Institute, which ran as a free hospital for 12 years. Today it is still going strong and emphasises the connection between the environment, a positive attitude and the healing journey. Like so many before him, Patch Adams believed strongly in the power of laughter in healing the body.

In stressful or painful situations, the body increases production of stress hormones such as cortisol and epinephrine. These cause a rise in heart rate and blood pressure. Research has proven that stress can also inhibit the body's immune system and weaken a person's defences, leaving them much more vulnerable to illness. Happily, new studies are indicating that humour just might have the opposite effect.

A Japanese study published several years ago in the *Journal of the American Medical Association* found that patients with skin welts caused by allergies experienced a dramatic reduction in symptoms when they watched Charlie Chaplin's comedic classic *Modern Times!* Another study in the United States was conducted by Maryland researchers reported that people with healthy hearts were more likely to laugh in humorous situations than people with heart disease. Of course, those with heart disease probably don't feel too much like laughing. However, as more and more research into the area takes place it is increasingly obvious that having a sense of humour makes you healthier.

You have probably witnessed this yourself. Perhaps you were really angry and then someone did something that made you burst out laughing. All the anger drains away in an instant. That release of such a potentially toxic emotion must be good for the body.

There can be no doubt that over the coming decades that scientific research will empirically prove the influence of the mind over the body. Norman Cousins and Bernie Siegel have been at the forefront of studies into just how important a positive attitude to treatment is to the recovery of the patient.

Norman Cousins laid the groundwork with his pioneering 1979 book, *Anatomy of an Illness as Perceived by the Patient*, describing how laughter helped reduce his pain from a debilitating joint disease called ankylosing spondylitis. Although Cousins passed away in 1990, his contribution to this area of understanding is significant and is an astonishing legacy for a brilliant and inspiring man.

There is no funding from the big pharmaceutical companies into this area of research – for obvious reasons. If it's discovered that one good belly laugh a day will keep the doctor away, what will they do with all that Prozac?

How to incorporate this wisdom into your life

Write down ten people that you admire and why you admire them. One of the easiest ways to change your mind is to change your physiology! If you find yourself in a bad emotional place – get out of the neighbourhood.

That means move your body – stand if you were previously sitting, go for a walk, go swimming – just do something. Because the body will release endorphins through physical exercise you will automatically break your pattern simply by moving your body. Experiments have shown that it is impossible to feel depressed if you are standing up tall, holding your head high, breathing deeply from your lower abdomen and smiling. Try it on now. Stand up straight, hold your head high, breathe deeply and smile until your face hurts. Even better, imagine something funny and laugh out loud like you have never laughed before. Isn't it true that you immediately start to feel differently?

Listening to uplifting music can also be a great way of getting out a negative frame of mind. Sound and music have a profound effect on our perception of the world. Even under general anaesthesia, sound is one of the last senses to go. Music is an expression of our human emotions – it can trigger emotional states and previously forgotten memories. The effect of sound is so profound that even sounds we think are inaudible have been proven to produce drastically altered emotional states and behaviours in individuals and groups.

When you think of the theme song from the classic movie *Rocky*, starring Sylvester Stallone, what images appear in your mind and how do they make you feel? How do those feelings differ from the theme song in *Jaws*, *The Titanic*, *Kill Bill* or even *Austin Powers*? The next time you feel down or upset put your favourite song on your MP3 player or your stereo and you will be amazed just how quickly you start to feel very differently.

Chapter 8

You play the hand you're dealt. I think the game's worthwhile.
~ Christopher Reeve

> Christopher Reeve was an actor, most famous for his role as Superman. His contribution to film and entertainment was nothing compared to his contribution following a horse riding accident that left him paralysed. He lobbied on behalf of spinal injury patients everywhere and was an outspoken advocate of stem cell research, which could hold the solution to spinal injuries. While he was certainly dealt a difficult hand, he played it with dignity and determination until his death in 2004.

Life isn't always easy – there can be no question about that. It's unpredictable and it's often hard to make sense of what happens. Some of the events in our journey end up being nothing more than minor irritants, while others are more like being hit by a Mack truck at 200 kph.

Regardless – we have to play the hand we are dealt.

Part of the process of coming to terms with whatever occurs in your life is to find a way to make sense of it. If science indicates that objective reality doesn't actually exist, it is very much up to us to create a reality that helps us move on and find some meaning. As W Mitchell so accurately points out, *'It's not what happens to you, it's what you do about it that matters'*.

I like to think of it as 'making chicken soup out of chicken shit'. And it is often in these times of desperation or perspiration that we accomplish our greatest achievements. We play the hand that we have been dealt and in so doing we stretch beyond the finite boundaries of probability and skill into the realm of possibility and inspiration.

For Christopher Reeve a random riding accident changed his life. Everything he was in terms of his career and how people perceived him vanished the instant he hit the ground. And yet he was able to muster his resources and master his own mind so as to find a reason to carry on. I'm sure becoming paralysed was not part of his life plan. I'm sure there must have been times that he was angry and bitter, but these feelings obviously didn't consume him.

The simple truth is that Christopher Reeves found himself in a wheelchair at just 43 years old. Nothing could be done to change that. There was no way to wind back the clock and no way to repair the damage. His condition was permanent. But his state of mind and any negative emotions he felt were temporary and 100% within his control. He had two options: (1) let the event consume his life and extinguish his spirit or (2) accept his condition and make the best use of his time and influence to advance science in the hope that someday others with spinal cord injuries might walk again. In many ways, he became more of a superhero after his accident than he had previously been in his film roles because he created a vision and a purpose that was bigger than the event that changed his life.

He accepted the cards he was dealt in the game of life and he played with the courage, determination and strength of character of a superhero. Perhaps Christopher himself said it best, *'I think a hero is an ordinary individual who finds the strength to persevere and endure in spite of overwhelming obstacles. They are the real heroes, and so are the families and friends who have stood by them'.*

Perhaps it is time that we all stood back and celebrated the superhero within ourselves and others. For me my greatest superhero was my grandfather …

He and my grandmother had four beautiful children – three of which predeceased them. Their first child, Mavis Annette, died of cancer at the age of six. My uncle's twin brother, Donald, died in the hospital after only a few days due to an infection. And my mother passed away suddenly at the age of only 43. If you met them, you would never have known their tragedy – they were incredibly loving, positive, genuine and supportive. They rarely complained about the hand that they had been dealt – their love and commitment to each other and their family was undeniable and they had a steadfast and unwavering belief in God that saw them through many hard times.

As a child, I didn't fully comprehend how amazing they both were – they had both suffered so much but yet they found a way to do the best that they could and make the most of what they did have. As someone who has had her own share of trials and tribulations, I am still in awe of my grandparents' strength, faith, tenacity and love. I cannot imagine what it would be like to lose a child – surely it has to be one of the most difficult things anyone could ever endure.

Satchel Paige once encouraged us to *'Work like you don't need the money, love like you've never been hurt, and dance like no one is watching'*. My grandparents lost three children and still found a way to love like they had never been hurt. I admire that so much!

And of course there is the flip side to all this. There are those that have been afforded every privilege that life has to offer and have still managed to make a spectacular mess of their lives. People who have been loved and supported by a loving family and have still managed to turn 'chicken soup into chicken shit!' Just think of those vacuous girls in Hollywood with small dogs in Gucci bags who have the money, power and connections to make a real contribution to the world and instead choose to party and shop.

Events mean nothing, the hand you are dealt in life is not a passage to nirvana, how you play the game is what matters. My grandparents taught me that lesson.

The years took an especially hard toll on my grandfather physically and emotionally but no matter what he endured, he remained an incredibly loving and spiritually strong man. He worked hard but he always put his family first. I don't ever remember a time when he was too busy to listen to or help me. He took a real interest in everything that I did and I cannot remember a single time when he lost his patience or yelled. His patience, support and encouragement were limitless.

One of my greatest regrets was not visiting him enough toward the end of his life. He loved to talk about his experiences working in Montreal in a factory during the war and his time with the Canadian Pacific Railway. Toward the end of his life, the events of 50 years ago were more vivid and real to him than what had happened a few days earlier.

He had lived a very full life but it was one fraught with unbelievable heartache and struggle. He had experienced and lived through more heartache than I would wish on my worst enemy. In the end, his heart grew too weak and the hundreds of small strokes that had robbed him of his memories and ability to care for himself, finally took their toll. Even though I knew it was wrong, I found it almost unbearable to visit him. I wanted him to be the man that he was when I young. I wanted him to be the one that I could run to for shelter, love and protection. I wanted him to be the one to take me in his loving arms and tell me that everything was going to be okay. Instead, it was me who was left to play the role of the caregiver and I felt so alone, so unequipped, and so inept.

I will admit that there have been many times in my life where I have felt overwhelmed, defeated or just plain sorry for myself. It's easy to focus on what you don't have or the things that have gone wrong – we just lose sight of the gifts and treasures that are still right in front of us.

More than once I have looked at the cards that I have been dealt and simply wanted to fold – to cash in, admit defeat and walk away. The one thing that keeps me going is the memory of my grandfather and his incredible life of contribution, commitment, love and fulfilment, despite formidable odds. By example, he taught me to believe that I can do or be anything, regardless of the hand that I have been dealt. I owe almost everything that I am or ever will be to the most incredible man that I have ever met and the only man I have ever truly trusted – Nicholas Kutinsky – my grandfather.

Did you know ... ?

On Friday 13 October 1972 Uruguayan Air Force Flight 571 crashed in the Andes carrying 45 people. Among the passengers were the Stella Maris College's 'Old Christians' rugby union team from Montevideo in Uruguay, destined for a match in Santigo, Chile. They never made that game. Instead they were plunged into a nightmare.

Twelve people died in the crash and three more never made it through the night. Several people were also missing. The remaining passengers faced terrible conditions; many had suffered injuries from the crash, including broken legs. They lacked equipment, suitable clothing or provisions to weather such a high altitude crash. After 11 days on the mountain, the survivors were devastated to hear a news report on a radio they had found the wreckage that the search had been called off. Piers Paul Read one of the survivors described the scene: 'The others who had clustered around [the radio] upon hearing the news, began to sob and pray, all except Parrado, who looked calmly up the mountains which rose to the west. Gustavo [Coco] Nicolich came out of the plane and, seeing their faces, knew what they had heard ... Nicolich climbed through the hole in the wall of suitcases and rugby shirts, crouched at the mouth of the dim tunnel, and looked at the mournful faces which were turned towards him. 'Hey boys,' he shouted, 'there's some good news! We just heard on the radio. They've called off the search.' Inside the crowded plane there was silence. As the hopelessness of their predicament enveloped them, they wept. 'Why the hell is that good news?' Paez shouted angrily at Nicholich. 'Because it means,' Nicholich said, 'that we're going to get out of here on our own.'

There was no food and no natural vegetation; in desperation they even tried to eat the leather of their shoes. They faced certain death from starvation unless they could do the unthinkable ... eventually they survived by collectively making a decision to eat flesh from the bodies of their dead comrades. A horrendous decision, no doubt made even harder by their deep religious faith. An avalanche killed a further eight of the original survivors. A small team eventually set out to find help. After a staggering 72 days on the mountain, the remaining survivors were airlifted to safety on the 23 December 1972. They were dealt a cruel and difficult hand and yet they played it the best they could and 16 survived to tell the tale.

How to incorporate this wisdom into your life

Do a personal SWOT analysis (strengths, weaknesses, opportunities and threats) on yourself so you can clarify what your cards are. Think back on the highs and lows of your life and write down what your greatest strengths are. Think in terms of skills, abilities, attitude, character traits, friends and family contacts. Write down all the positive things in your life. Then, write down your vulnerabilities. Make a note of the things that do, or could potentially, limit you. But remember often our weaknesses are just a different side of the same coin. For example, being dedicated and hard working is a strength, however, it is also vulnerability when it is used as a way to avoid intimate relationships or of putting off your family and friends. That same trait can also be a weakness if it's not tempered by balance.

Knowing yours strengths and weaknesses puts you in a position to assess the opportunities and threats that they pose for you in your life. Getting clear about them allows you to really capitalise on the hand you were dealt instead of wishing you could change it.

Chapter 9

I like coincidences. They make me wonder about destiny, and whether free will is an illusion or just a matter of perspective. They let me speculate on the idea of some master plan that, from time to time, we're allowed to see out of the corner of our eye. ~ Chuck Sigars

Chuck Sigars is a freelance writer and the author of 'The World According to Chuck'. He also writes a weekly newspaper column called 'Chuck's World' that runs in small papers in Washington.

I have often been fascinated by coincidence and what it means, so when I found this quote, I smiled, because it encapsulates beautifully the intrigue and mystery behind coincidence. I strongly believe that there is no such thing as a coincidence. If I look back on my own life I can see that apparent random coincidences have more often than not led to some deep connection or guidepost in my own journey.

In my hometown in rural Canada, my best friend Tabatha's brother was murdered exactly one week after my mother. The circumstances were completely unrelated yet we found ourselves in the same awful place. Although the concurrent event was one I'd not wish on my worst enemy, in a strange way it allowed us to support each other through a terrible time and become even closer in the process. There was an unspoken understanding between us – a connection, insight and empathy that would not have existed if it were not for these events. Where many others simply could not find the words to express their concern and support, Tabatha didn't need to. She understood my pain – the sense of helplessness and despair – and she graciously and effortlessly carried me when I thought that I could not go on. And I hope I did the same for her.

For Tabatha, her brother's death was the catalyst that caused her to go back to university to complete her degree in business. At the time, I was in an unhealthy relationship with a guy I couldn't count on and she helped extricate me from that. She resumed studies in September that year and we lived together for almost eight months. Having her support made all the difference to me – especially when I was articling for law, going through all the criminal trials and my health was suffering due to severe depression, insomnia and extreme weight loss. She was the one person who completely understood how I felt and on whom I could count. We were best friends before this ever happened and going through this cemented the bond between us. I consider her and her family to be my family and there is nothing that I would not do for her.

Many years later, I experienced this phenomenon again in a profound way. While representing my retail business at an International Women's conference in Washington DC, I met a woman who owned a cosmetics business in Australia. She sat immediately in front of me – if it had not been for the speaker suggesting that we all stand up and introduce ourselves to the women around us, we may not have met each other. We kept in touch for months afterwards via email and I was eventually offered a position with her company in Melbourne, Australia in 2005.

That allowed me to make a new start here in Australia. I landed in Melbourne with two suitcases full of my belongings, really only knowing one person. And I've never looked back – absolutely everything fell into place – job, home, friends etc. In fact, I made the decision and moved to Australia in only 9 days. It was one of the biggest decisions I have ever made and one of the quickest. I felt afraid and unsure, but I did it anyway. Interestingly enough, this all happened against the backdrop of my seven-year marriage failing and my business going under due to an inability to find external financing. At the time, the proverbial tree that I was on was definitely on fire and this chance meeting in Washington DC presented me with the opportunity to jump to a new tree, albeit 20,000km away!

I have no idea what the odds of these events might be? Would it be more or less than being dealt a flush in a poker game, running into a friend you haven't seen in 25 years or winning a million dollars in a lottery? Perhaps this is not even the right question to ask? What I do know, however, is that when you live your life with an awareness and appreciation of 'coincidences' and open yourself up to the divine guidance and support within them, you connect to a source of energy, direction and purpose that is truly magical and life changing.

Did you know ... ?

In his book *Synchronicity: The Bridge Between Matter and Mind*, Dr F David Peat, a physicist at Queen's University in Canada, asserted that coincidences were actually *'flaws in the fabric of reality'*. He believed that these occurrences that were so unusual and so psychologically significant as to be outside the field of chance alone revealed that our thought process is much more intimately connected to the physical world than has been previously considered.

Another great believer in the concept of coincidences and their power to help guide us is Dr Deepak Chopra. In his book *Synchro Destiny: Harnessing the infinite power of coincidence to create miracles*, he says that, 'A coincidence is a clue to intention of the universal spirit, and as such is rich with significance'. Coincidence is the universe's way of guiding you toward your destiny through 'acausal nonlocal connection' that is, incidents that are connected to each other without having a direct cause and effect relationship. Chopra goes on to say, *'We cannot even imagine the complex forces behind every event that occurs in our lives. There's a conspiracy of coincidences that weave the web of karma or destiny and creates an individual's personal life – mine, or yours'.*

Coincidences are all around us – some of them are trivial, while others have a way of demanding our attention and intrigue. Regardless of the significance or meaning, what these events do have in common is our intense desire as humans to explain them or attribute a connection. Oftentimes the illusory nature of this process only serves to intensify our need and desire to achieve it. The more the meaning and connection is hidden, the more energetically we attempt to uncover it.

Sometimes we are so busy forcing our way through life that we don't notice the little signs and nudges in different directions. When we do notice them, we try in earnest to over-analyse and impose meaning, and in doing so often miss the point of why the serendipitous event happened in the first place. I truly believe that coincidences are the universe's way of guiding us toward things, events, people and situations that can help us to fulfil our destiny and live with purpose. The meaning or connection is not the most important part – it's about being awake and open to the guidance and support of the universe and trusting on a deep inner level that all you need will be provided. If you can let go of your need to know every little detail and take your hands off the wheel, the ride can become a truly magical and effortless one.

How to incorporate this wisdom into your life

Instead of brushing coincidences aside as nothing more than random chance, take notice of them. Suppose for a moment that seemingly random events are in fact gentle nudges in a particular direction – what direction might that be? Perhaps you hear someone's name from the past repeated in a variety of strange circumstances. Could this mean that you should get in touch with that person? Perhaps you find yourself drawn to a particular course of study and suddenly meet strangers who start talking about how they did that very same course. Begin to pay attention to the people and ideas that come across your path.

If you find yourself struggling against life and you feel as though you are always having to push to get anything done, perhaps it's such a struggle because it's not actually your path. Take some time out to think and connect to what your hopes and dreams are. Start to pay attention to the signs leading you to or away from your goals – you may begin to discover insights and direction toward something much more fulfilling that alters your life completely. Begin a daily journal and keep track of words, phrases, people, events, dreams and things that are showing up as coincidences in your life. Start to track the recurring themes – the goal is not to evaluate but to gain insight.

Often coincidences happen to remind us of our own part in the events that occur. For example, you may dislike your boss and decide to get a new job. A few months into your new job you are flabbergasted to find out that your new boss is exactly the same as your old one, only even more irritating! You may just think this is bad luck and decide to move on again. Only at the third job, you discover the exact same thing.

This type of coincidence is actually not a coincidence at all – it is a reminder to you that the only real common denominator in all their situations is you. It is a prompt for you to change some aspect of your own character so that you will stop attracting those types of employers!

Chapter 10

You control your future, your destiny. What you think about comes about.
By recording your dreams and goals on paper, you set in motion the process
of becoming the person you most want to be. Put your future in good hands
– your own. ~ Mark Victor Hansen

Mark Victor Hansen is perhaps most well known for his contribution
to the *Chicken Soup of the Soul* book series. He is a prolific author
and was a successful entrepreneur before turning his attention to
motivational speaking and the field of human potential.

For years, speakers in the personal development and motivational
industry have touted a Yale study as evidence that goal setting
substantially increases success. The story goes something like this: In
1953, researchers surveyed Yale's graduating senior class to determine
how many of them had written, specific goals for their future
careers. The answer was 3%. Twenty years later, researchers polled
the surviving members of the class and uncovered that the 3% had
accumulated more financial wealth than the other 97% combined.

As far as impressive and compelling evidence goes, this Ivy League
success story appears to prove a direct cause and effect relationship
between goal setting and financial success. If you have read any
books in this area or attended any seminars, my bet is that you have
already heard this story more than once. America's top minds and
consultants – Zig Ziglar, Brian Tracy, Jay Rifenbary and Anthony
Robbins have all quoted this study in order to substantiate their case
for goal setting. There is only one small problem – it probably didn't
happen.

In 1996 Lawrence Tabak, a Kansas City based writer tried to uncover the evidence for this powerful study. After contacting each of the above noted speakers, the secretary of the Class of 1953 and a Research Associate at Yale, absolutely no proof was uncovered to substantiate that this research in fact ever took place.

At the end of the day, it doesn't really matter whether the study occurred or not. When you read 'Did you know?' below you'll understand that goal setting works because of forces far greater than Ivy League studies!

You have to know what it is you are seeking to achieve in life otherwise it's so easy to drift aimlessly. Years pass like days and next thing you know 20 years have passed and you've still not finished that novel that you started to write, not gone back to school to get that degree, not sorted your financial affairs, never bothered to get around to learning a second language etc.

Thomas Stanley, author of *The Millionaire Woman Next Door* asked female millionaires, 'Do you have a clearly defined set of daily, weekly, monthly, annual and lifetime goals?'

For every 100 female millionaires who said 'no', there were 261 that said 'yes'. And of the 100 who said 'no', many of these were already retirees. The fact remains that the vast majority of self-made women in this study were goal setters and I think it is fair to assume that this basic principle would also apply to men.

I very clearly remember when I first started to get serious about setting goals.

I had already achieved a high level of success in my professional career. I was in the top 2–3% of female income earners in the country – I held two professional designations, worked in a senior sales and marketing position with a leading national retailer and had become a specialist in loyalty and direct marketing. But yet, I longed for more – more success and challenge in my career and in leading a team, a better work life balance, financial freedom, more satisfying personal relationships and a renewed focus on my health. Plus I also had a dream to be a published author and speaker.

In December 2006, I decided to set some specific goals for myself. I have always considered myself a very driven and successful person, yet I had rarely written a goal down on paper in my life. I decided back then to write some goals – not just career goals but goals for every aspect of my life – personal, social, financial, career, health etc. These goals were more than just a little 'stretch'. They were ambitious and aggressive – goals that I would not have been able to achieve were it not for the tools and techniques that I am going to share with you in this chapter.

For example, one of the goals was about my desire to triple my net worth within 12 months. Now you have to understand that at the time I set the goal, I did not make enough money at my job in a year to reach my goal. I'm sure you would agree, that sounds like a bit of a stretch! However, I actually achieved that goal in just nine months.

By utilising specific goal setting tools and semantics, I opened up channels of income and revenue that I never imagined possible. Once I got clear about the 'what', without needing to be clear about the 'how', I was able to attract people and circumstances into my life that made my goals possible. And I can also tell you that out of the nine goals that I wrote in December of 2006, I achieved eight by November of 2007. As at that date of writing this book, only one goal is still outstanding … and I haven't given up on it yet.

There is one last thing that I want to touch on in the context of goal setting – it is the distinction between goals and dreams. And it is this distinction that I believe makes all the difference. From my perspective, traditional goal setting seems like a very clinical exercise. Pick up any self-help or business book and it will tell you how to set SMART goals – specific, measurable, achievable, realistic and time bound. While I agree with the necessity of these basic factors, I also think it is absolutely crucial to incorporate the element of dreams and the imagination.

By their very nature, dreams are illogical, irrational, non-sequential, without specific steps and difficult to measure. However, it is my observation that too many of us get limited in our goal setting by the constraints of our own imagination. We would all like to make an extra $10,000 a year but we have no powerful, compelling reason 'WHY'. What exactly would you do with another $10,000? That is the critical question to ask yourself … Connect with 'what' or 'why' and the 'how' will make itself known to you in the most miraculous ways.

Did you know ... ?

The reason goal setting works is biological. There is a part of your brain called the Reticular Activating System (RAS). It has several functions but the one that is most relevant to this discussion is its filtration system. In Chapter 4 we talked about being bombarded with millions of bits of information per second, and that what we become aware of depends on our beliefs and values etc. The RAS is the mechanism that deletes the vast majority of information from your conscious awareness.

Simply stated, that is why knowing specifically what it is you're trying to achieve is so important because it consciously puts those things onto your internal radar. And once they are on your radar, your mind will filter for and locate information, resources and opportunities that will allow you to meet your goal. This is why you can quite happily go through life not noticing pregnant woman and then suddenly when you decide to start a family, you begin to notice them everywhere. That conscious decision of wanting to start a family put the goal on your internal radar system and you will begin to notice pregnant woman around every corner. The whole world will appear to be breeding!

The world is the same today as it was yesterday, except that yesterday you had not made a decision to start a family. The single act of making that choice has activated your RAS and now you notice new information and access to new knowledge that you were previously oblivious to. Goal setting works because it is like giving yourself a good kick up the RAS!

Even so, $10,000 is not a huge stretch in today's terms. In my experience most of us never dare to aspire to double or triple our income? Why is that? The missing element in my estimation is the realm of dreams and imagination. By its very nature, a dream is something that is potentially unrealistic. However, dreams are incredibly powerful and compelling because they are about who you are becoming, not who you are now. Dreams and imagination lie within the domain of the subconscious mind. By incorporating this additional element into the goal setting process, we connect to the infinite resourcefulness of the subconscious and ignite a passion that will inspire and drive us towards our goals.

How to incorporate this wisdom into your life

Whilst you need the capacity to dream you also need to be able to move that vision from the ethereal to the material and that is where my goal setting methodology comes in - MY RESULT:

M – Measurable result, how will you know when you get there? What exactly does the end step look like?

Y – Why? For what purpose/intention do you want it? Do not be afraid to dream BIG here!

R – Realistic and achievable, however, do not be afraid to set a longer term goal that is a stretch or a challenge.

E – Ecological – is it good for you, others and the planet?

S – Specific, clear and concise goals – ensure you subconscious mind knows what it is working towards.

U – You have it now. The goal must be written in the present, as if you have it now and signed by you.

L – Looking toward your goal, not moving away from what you do not want, action-oriented.

T – Time bound, must have a specific achievement date.

With each of the above in mind, select an area of your life that you would like to focus on and write a goal for – family and home, career and finances, personal relationships, health, mental and educational, social and cultural or spiritual and ethical. Complete the following template:

Today's date_____

Achievement date_____

It is now, <u>\<insert achievement date\></u>_____and I <u>\<your</u>

<u> name\></u>_____ am/have_____

_____

_____

_____

_____

This now comes to fruition or something even better and I give thanks to the abundance of the universe for my incredible gifts, health, abundance and good fortune.

Signed_____

For example, I may be interested in changing jobs and making more money in my career. In order to open myself to new and exciting possibilities that are well suited to my values, personality etc, I would write the goal as follows:

Today's date:_ Jan 1, 2008

Achievement date:_ April 15, 2008

It is now, April 15, 2008 and I Rhondalynn have a job/profession that suits my personality, skills, values and characteristics that pays me more than $200,000/year. In this new position, I feel empowered, supported, challenged, enthusiastic, respected and mentally stimulated. I am sitting in my new office and saying out loud how much I love what I do and the people that I work with. Until I find this new opportunity, I give 100% to my current position.

This now comes to fruition or something even better than I imagined and I give thanks to the abundance of the universe for my incredible gifts, health, abundance and good fortune.

Signed Rhondalynn

In the goal setting process above, it is important to really make the goal come alive in your own words. How do you imagine what you want? What do you see, feel, hear, smell or taste? Really connect with the emotions and the end step of what you will be doing at the exact moment the goal is achieved.

The more clear you are about 'what' and 'why', the more powerful this process will be for you. Let the 'how' take care of itself. Don't forget to dream BIG! It has been said that people often overestimate what they can do in a year but grossly underestimate what they can do in ten years. In my experience working with clients, the bigger and more amazing the goal, the more motivated and excited they are to strive towards it.

Chapter 11

It's in your moments of decision that your destiny is shaped.
~ Anthony Robbins

> Anthony Robbins is an American peak performance coach, author and professional presenter in the field of human potential. One of his programs involves a fire walk and while he has his critics, there can be no doubt that Tony has been the catalyst for change for millions of people around the world.

Something magical happens when you make a real decision. Once you make a decision, and I mean a proper decision, the universe seems to conspire in your favour. The truth is most of us rarely actually decide anything – not in the true sense of the word. The word 'decide' comes from the Latin *decidere* which literally means to cut off. So an actual decision is one where you cut off from any other course of action or alternative. You block the exits and escape hatches and move forward single-mindedly in the direction of your choice.

Most of us make a 'decision' today, knowing that tomorrow we can change our mind, backtrack or simply do nothing. That isn't a decision. Unless you take action immediately towards your goal, you haven't really decided … you are merely thinking about it.

The decisions that Robbins is talking about are the ones that happen at times of absolute crisis. Something happens … and it is the straw that literally breaks the camel's back. We reach the point of no return and something inside of us snaps. Enough is enough. There is no going back.

I reached that point myself in the late months of 1998. I had backed myself into a corner professionally and I had changed jobs several times in the previous three years and I was still unsatisfied. In my heart, I longed to make a real contribution and to be challenged and inspired both intellectually and creatively. I was being paid well as a taxation lawyer and chartered accountant but my career wasn't meeting my needs on a deeper level. I had committed 12 years of my life to university education and articling – I couldn't just walk away from that. People would think I was insane. What would my family and friends say? How would I explain this to my husband? And worse, how was I going to figure out what I actually wanted to do?

I felt trapped, embarrassed and terrified. The stage was set for me to make the decision that would alter the course of my life forever.

I began to notice that I started thinking a lot about an idea that I had been toying with for more than a year. More and more women were entering the workforce in a professional capacity – doctors, lawyers, accountants, engineers etc. Many of these women had delayed starting a family in order to pursue their education and establish themselves in their respective careers. As these executives approached their early and mid-30s many of them decided to start families and they openly discussed issues that were important and pressing to them. A common theme at that time was the lack of professional, fashionable and flattering maternity clothing. Most of the women that I knew simply wouldn't be caught dead in most of what was for sale in mainstream maternity retailers.

I had a really strong feeling about this particular business and I identified closely with the vision/purpose – to help women who were expecting maintain their professional appearance and feel good about their changing bodies. The only drawback was I knew nothing about starting a retail business, let alone catering to pregnant professional women. I didn't even have children of my own.

In early 1999, in a moment of temporary insanity, I decided to leave a lucrative and stable career to venture off into the uncertain world of small business ownership committing all of my financial resources to the project. I opened the retail store itself within two months of leaving my job behind and had the online and catalogue divisions up shortly thereafter. For me, momentum was the key – once the decision was made, I moved full-steam ahead with my 30, 90 and 120-day action plans. In 2001, the Retail Sales Council of Canada named me Innovative Retailer of the Year (for businesses with less than $10 million of sales) for my marketing, advertising and e-commerce accomplishments.

But what if you are reading this thinking, 'That's great but I have no idea what business or career path I want to take?' Or you may need to make a decision about your health or personal relationships but you have been unsure or just plain reluctant to make a decision that would cut off your escape routes. Either way, it doesn't really matter. In my experience, the simple act of making a decision and taking action toward that outcome, even if it's baby steps, will cause your mind to seek out opportunities and guide you towards your destined path.

George Lucas, the famous filmmaker, decided at a young age that he would be a millionaire by the time he was 30. Initially the route he chose to fulfil that ambition was to become a famous racecar driver. However, a near fatal accident in his souped-up car around the time of his high school graduation quickly changed his mind. Instead he attended community college and developed a passion for the safer pursuit of filmmaking, later enrolling in University of Southern California film school. As a result of his decision to become a millionaire and his dedication to be the best at everything he did, Lucas did in fact become a millionaire by the time he was 30. He was 28 when he made his first million and he went on to create a legacy of films that will be remembered and treasured for many years.

Similarly, at the age of eight, Tiger Woods stunned the audience when he declared in a TV interview that he would become the World's #1 golfer and that he would break all of Jack Nicholas's records. Even at a young age, his focus, dedication and obsession allowed him to channel all of his efforts and action towards improving his game. At the age of 22, Tiger realised his goal of becoming the #1 golfer in the world and he has gone on to break the records held by golf's greatest legends.

When you study the lives of the most successful people in history – Donald Trump, Warren Buffet, Lance Armstrong, Anthony Robbins, Richard Branson – you will discover that many of them had a dream to accomplish something truly remarkable. What separates these great minds from the average person is not the goal, but rather the decision. We all have goals and aspirations, but few of us achieve them. The key lies in your ability to make a real decision and take immediate action. The civil rights movement in America was started by one little decision by Rosa Louise Parks. Her refusal to surrender her seat to a white male passenger on a Montgomery, Alabama bus on 1 December 1955 triggered a wave of protests that reverberated throughout the United States. Her quiet act of courage changed America and altered the course of history.

Did you know ... ?

New science is discovering that our focused intention does impact the results we achieve. When we learn to master our intention and consistently direct our attention and focus toward a particular outcome, the chances of that occurring is increased far beyond random chance. If we are always changing our minds and never really committing to anything, then how can the forces that are quite clearly at work ever know what it is we are trying to achieve?

Dr William Tiller of Stanford University is a leading figure in the study of intention and how our thoughts interact with the environment. He has shown just how powerful our thoughts are. In one experiment he had seasoned meditators focus their intention on black boxes with the instruction to 'increase the pH of the water by 1%.' Now considering a rise in pH of 1% in the human body would be fatal, this result was significant enough to illustrate it could not occur naturally. These boxes were then placed next to water taken from the same source. All the boxes that had been meditated over did indeed show an increase in the pH of the water. The control boxes showed no change. It has therefore been proven that what we choose and what we think about does have a very real effect on what we experience.

Look back in your own life ... are you able to pick out two or three decisions that completely changed the course of your life? Perhaps you decided to go travelling before going to college or perhaps you decided to get married or divorced? Major events in your life occur at some point following a clear-cut decision. Those decisions may not always be good ones and they may not always lead in the direction you want but you always have the power to change. Regret is a useless indulgence. If you are not happy with parts of your life right now, the best time to make a new decision is today. In the words of a great man, Theodore Roosevelt, *'In any moment of decision the best thing you can do is the right thing, the next best thing is the wrong thing, and the worst thing you can do is nothing'.*

You have the power right now to make a decision and move toward what you want in life. Life is not a dress rehearsal. Now some of you might be thinking 'Of course, I know that'. However, the truth is this – until you DO, you don't really KNOW. And the only pertinent question that you should ask yourself is, 'Am I really living, making decisions and moving forward, or am I still just thinking about it?

Part of the problem in today's modern world is that everything is disposable – including decisions. As a result, our decision-making muscle is weak because we rarely exercise our ability to make a proper decision. Instead we see how things go. The rise in communication mediums has meant that we no longer need to make decisions about simple things like what time to meet friends. Instead we text them with instructions minutes before we're supposed to meet. Choices are much more fluid – just look at the increasing divorce rate.

But we truly are doing ourselves a huge disservice by not making commitments and following through on them, especially when you consider what quantum physics is indicating about the nature of reality.

Our life and the quality of that life is dependent not on our personal circumstance, genetic disposition, environment or any other external factor. It is dependent on the quality of our internal world. In turn, the quality of our internal world is very much dependent on the decisions we make. The quality of our questions affect our decisions. The quality of our decisions affect our actions. And the quality of our actions affect the quality of our results and ultimately our lives.

At the end of the day, if you have decided something in some aspect of your life but have not yet taken action … you haven't really decided anything, you are still just thinking about it.

How to incorporate this wisdom into your life

Anthony Robbins talks of a very simple four-step process that he calls the *Ultimate Success Formula*. And it is a great way to begin making decisions and moving toward your chosen outcome.

1. First decide what it is you want.
2. Take action.
3. Notice whether or not your action is moving you toward or further away from your goal.
4. Change the approach until you get what you desire.

Decision-making is a habit that you need to develop. If you've got out the habit of making real decisions then you need to practice on little things and get used to the feeling again. Make a list of ten things that you know you should do but have been putting off doing. Write down a time by which you will complete each one and take action today to complete at least one.

Chapter 12

Whatever you can do or dream you can, begin it. Boldness has genius, power and magic in it. Begin it now. ~ Johann Wolfgang Von Goethe

Goethe was a famous German writer, poet, novelist, dramatist, theorist, painter and natural scientist! His vast knowledge in a variety of fields earned him a formidable reputation and his play Faust is considered one of the best literary achievements of all time. His scientific work influenced Darwin and his contribution to philosophy is immeasurable.

When I'm doing consultations with clients, one of the things I am constantly brought back to is this quote. When I first meet someone for a session and we discuss what it is they want to change or achieve, more often than not, one of two things will happen. The first is that the individual may find it really difficult to dream big dreams. If they are able to get past that first hurdle, they will immediately say how difficult it will be. And every time I am reminded of this quote.

Goethe doesn't say, *'Whatever you can do or dream you can, plan it, work out every single detail of then make it happen'*.

He simply says, 'Begin it!'

You have to dream it and then get moving. So often we curtail our dreams and hopes for the future because from the vantage point of NOW, it seems improbable or even impossible. But the two vital ingredients to change are dreaming and commitment. Planning is important and has its place but you cannot wait to have it all worked out before you begin. If you do, you will never start anything.

Goethe's actually said quite a bit more than just the snippet quoted at the beginning of this chapter …

'Until one is committed, there is hesitancy, the chance to draw back, always ineffectiveness. Concerning all acts of initiative and creation, there is one elementary truth the ignorance of which kills countless ideas and splendid plans: that the moment one definitely commits oneself, then providence moves too. All sorts of things occur to help one that would never otherwise have occurred. A whole stream of events issues from the decision, raising in one's favor all manner of unforeseen incidents, meetings and material assistance which no man could have dreamed would have come his way. Whatever you can do or dream you can, begin it. Boldness has genius, power and magic in it. Begin it now'.

In the previous chapter we explored the importance of making a decision. That is amplified here. Once that choice is made and you are committed, people, resources and prospects materialise that would not otherwise have appeared. You don't have to know the 'how' when you commit to a course of action. Once you know the 'why', the 'how' will take care of itself. But first, you must make the decision and BEGIN IT!

When you move toward your choice, 'providence moves too'. The 'how' will begin to unfold. You will find a path; new people will turn up in your life, opportunities will present themselves in ways that will leave you in little doubt of the magic Goethe talked about.

I decided in December 2006 that I wanted to write and publish my first book and I committed that goal to paper immediately. I did not have the first clue about writing a book, and I knew even less about actually publishing one, but I was 100% committed to this dream. I began organising my thoughts and sketching out a rough outline for the chapters. As the skeleton began to take shape, I delved further into research and commenced reading every book I could find on personal development and the science of how our mind actually works.

After reaching a point where I had good chunks of the book laid out in outline form I hit the wall in terms of knowing where to go next. But I'd committed to my vision and providence moved … I found a website where professional writers were offering their services for hire. I received an overwhelming interest back from a variety of writers from around the world. Most importantly, that website led me to one particular writer who helped me with this project. She had already ghostwritten several books in the personal development industry and was thus very familiar with my intended subject matter. Also, she and I had an instant connection – I felt a sense of affinity with her and a strong belief that she would allow my words, emotions and stories to come through in a way that would be authentic, memorable and inspiring.

Around the same time I was also invited to an investment seminar in Melbourne given by Peter Spann. I remember being particularly excited because Denis Waitley, international best-selling author and speaker was scheduled to appear. After purchasing a copy of his book, *Seeds of Greatness,* I waited in line with hundreds of others to have it autographed. When it came time for Denis to sign my book, he paused and commented on my unique name. Without hesitation, I piped in and exclaimed 'You will definitely be hearing it again very soon as I am writing my first book this year and know in my heart it will be a best seller.'

Even I was shocked at the words that had come out of my mouth. But I had put them out there and there was absolutely no going back now. To my delight Denis pulled out his business card, handed it to me and offered his assistance in achieving my dream. I had just met one of my all-time favourite authors in the world – someone whom I admired and respected greatly – and he had actually volunteered to help me.

Towards the end of 2007 I began to turn my attention towards the task of finding a publisher. I was having coffee with a very good friend of mine – someone I had known for years – and the topic of my book and a publishing deal came up. I began explaining the various concerns I had over finding the right publisher, negotiating to retain the rights to produce an audio version of the book, gaining solid trade distribution and PR opportunities. What I didn't know at the time was that Marlene had actually worked in the publishing industry for Penguin in America, prior to being transferred to Australia with Disney. She understood exactly what the issues were and offered her services to help me negotiate the right deal when the time came.

At the time I committed myself to the dream of writing my book, I had no idea what I would write about, how it would actually come together or where I would find a publisher. I only knew the 'why' – I wanted to make a difference by sharing my stories and inspiring others to move beyond their perceived limitations – and I let the universe take care of the 'how'.

Don't wait until all the circumstances are perfect before making a commitment. You can't wait until all the *i*'s have been dotted and *t*'s have been crossed before taking action. There is never a right time – right now is the only time there is. Don't worry about making mistakes – it's a certainty that you will – but remember that any decision is better than no decision.

Did you know ... ?

Inertia is a fundamental principal of classic physics that, put simply, states that 'A body in motion tends to remain in motion, a body at rest tends to remain at rest.' Inertia is the force that stops things from moving. The hardest part of moving anything – whether it's you toward your dreams or a football toward the goal – is the start. You have to break out of the condition of inertia and once you do then momentum kicks in and each subsequent movement becomes progressively easier until eventually it becomes impossible to stop!

It is the same with making decisions.

The observant reader will notice that some of the ideas put forward in various chapters appear contradictory. Some of life's most important lessons are! The world is full of dichotomies or opposing truths that can confuse those looking for 'one right way'. For example, we talk about the ease of being on the right path. Where bizarre coincidences confirm the correct way, and that when we are doing what we should be doing there is a simplicity and ease to the process. And yet on the other hand we talk about the necessity to meet and surmount obstacles. Both are true. The same can be said for this idea that you don't have to have all the answers – you just have to start. On the other hand, planning is a very important part of any process. It allows you to refine the process. But it appears contradictory to the idea that we should just jump in feet first and make the rest up as we go.

Unfortunately I have no definitive answer for this. Life's dichotomies are all true. That's what makes life so interesting and frustrating at times. You have to get a feel for what's happening around you so that you can judge for yourself when obstacles are just tests or a sign to change direction. Only you will know. And similarly if you continue jumping into things without any thought and ignore the planning stage once you've taken the plunge, then you will almost certainly pay the price.

What Goethe was referring to specifically was the benefit of movement. It's so easy to sit on the fence and vacillate but nothing will ever get done. Get off the fence one-way or the other; get on the pitch and into the game instead of bitching from the terraces! Then at least you have the opportunity to change your tactics as the game progresses. No one likes a whinger that is only ever happy sitting on the sidelines shouting about how much better they could do. Make a decision right now and get into the game. You have to overcome your trepidation and get moving toward the things you want in your life. Then and only then will you find solutions, attract resources and uncover opportunities that have the power to transform your world.

How to incorporate this wisdom into your life

The key phrase in Goethe's quote is 'Begin it now'. Not 'begin it tomorrow' or 'begin it later' or 'begin it next week' – 'Begin it NOW'.

Think of something that you really want. Perhaps you would really like a promotion or a new job. What can you do right now that will break the inertia of that choice and get you into action? You could immediately go online and look at online job sites. After scouring the sites you could update your resume and submit it to a recruitment agency. You could phone your friend that has been talking about a possible new role in their business.

Whatever it is – Begin it now!

Chapter 13

A man who becomes conscious of the responsibility he bears toward a human being who affectionately waits for him, or to an unfinished work, will never be able to throw away his life. He knows the 'why' for his existence, and will be able to bear almost any 'how'. ~ Viktor Frankl

Viktor Frankl was an Austrian neurologist, psychiatrist and the author of a little book called *Man's Search for Meaning*. And if anyone should know about finding meaning in difficult times it has to be Viktor Frankl. Not only were most of his family murdered in the gas chambers of Nazi Germany, he witnessed unspeakable horrors over many years before his eventual release. He went on to develop logotherapy and existential therapy, which have helped millions of people to find meaning in their own lives.

Sometimes life isn't pleasant, it almost certainly isn't fair. I know that from my own experiences and from seeing so many others go through terrible grief and pain. For years after my mum's death I just couldn't piece things together. Nothing made any sense and if someone had told me to find some positive meaning in it all, I think I would have punched them!

Personal tragedy and pain is a uniquely individual journey and no one has the right to pass judgement or make suggestions about how you should or shouldn't be handling it. There are two different people in the world – those that have lost someone close to them and those that have not … yet.

The latter can never understand the anguish of the former and I sometimes wonder if they should ever try. I'm not saying that we shouldn't comfort each other but offering personal development quips about looking for the positive side is probably not a wise move if you hope to remain upright! I am always surprised just how freely people offer up their advice especially when they have no idea what the other person is going through because they have never experienced anything remotely similar.

The paradox of course is that somehow you do eventually have to find a way to cope and move on, but often we have to arrive at that conclusion ourselves! I remember reading *Man's Search for Meaning* by Frankl and being amazed by him and his journey. How do you witness unimaginable horror, lose your family and somehow find 'meaning' to help you move on and take a step forward?

You do exactly what he suggests. Become conscious of some bigger responsibility. For Frankl, his bigger responsibility was to humanity. He wanted to survive so that he could tell the world about what happened in the hope that it would never happen again. He needed to survive to document his research and therapy – tested out on his fellow prisoners in their darkest of hours. He found a good enough 'why' to take another step when all he really felt like doing was giving up and checking out.

I could relate to that. At least the wanting to give up bit! I had earned an articling position at the top law firm in Calgary just before my mother died. She died just before my graduation in April of 1992, and I started work at the law firm in June of that same year.

I made the decision to carry on as planned, primarily to create a reason to get out of bed. I had lost a lot of weight going from about 130lbs down to 98lbs. I was having difficulty sleeping and was on anti-depressants and sleeping pills for most of that year. In my law school graduation photos, I look absolutely terrible – almost emaciated. I felt like everyone was tiptoeing around me – for the most part, I think they just didn't know what to say, so many of them said nothing.

People avoided me and I understand that they simply didn't have the words to express how they felt and it almost certainly made them feel uncomfortable. This was such a lonely time for me. As an aside, if you ever find yourself in a position where someone you know has been touched by tragedy, try to say something, even if it's just, 'I really don't know what to say but I'm so sorry to hear about your situation and I am here any time you need to talk.'

I did what I had to do in order to create some illusion of normality. I felt responsibility to my employer to get up each day, take a shower and show up to work. It wasn't a conscious thing, but looking back, I can see now that finding a little 'why' helped me take a new step forward each day. There was a routine and purpose to my life and people expected me to be there – in many ways that helped me move forward. To be honest, there are whole chunks of that year that I simply do not remember at all. I don't think I was a huge asset to the firm but having that job was a lifeline to me.

It wasn't an easy year and I'm certainly not going to tell you otherwise. It was incredibly difficult and trying – especially since some of the people that I worked with were critical of my being there at all. They felt that I should have taken time off – perhaps even travelled overseas! I found this notion completely ridiculous. I was physically unwell, seriously underweight, depressed and had for all intents and purposes lost my entire immediate family. Exactly where did they think that I should have gone? Strangely enough, I wasn't in the mood for a European holiday.

I won't pretend that I never contemplated ending my own life. There were many times I wished that a car or a bus would just veer off the road and run me over. The loss and the senselessness of it all were just unbearable for me. I was haunted by the terror and trauma of what her last moments must have been like. Even at what was undoubtedly the 'bottom' for me, I knew intuitively that I had to try to create some meaning to live. That meaning was just getting up and knowing that I had somewhere that I had to be each day. I also didn't want to let down my best friend (she needed my support at that time as well) and I didn't want to cause any more pain for my grandparents.

Strange as it sounds, I also had pets that needed me and I wanted to make sure that I did all that I could to make sure that justice was served in the court proceedings. I focused on my responsibility to others to help get myself through the immediate crisis. And it made all the difference.

Benjamin Franklin said, *'While we may not be able to control all that happens to us, we can control what happens inside us'*. Our life is not dictated by a collection of events, it is dictated by the meaning we ascribe to those events.

Did you know ... ?

Oprah Winfrey was fired from one of her first jobs as a television reporter and told, *'She wasn't fit for TV'*. What meaning do you think she ascribed to that defining moment? Do you think she went back to her apartment and told herself that she should just give up and get a desk job?

After his first performance on the Grand Ole Opry, Elvis Presley was banned from returning and told, *'You ain't going nowhere son!'* At that crucial moment in his career, do you think the King of Rock n' Roll created a meaning of defeat and limitation? Did he simply give up?

After Fred Astaire's first screen test, the testing director of MGM sent a memo that simply said, *'Can't act! Slightly bald! Can dance a little'*. Did Fred take the testing director's opinion to heart and simply give up or did he keep a copy of that memo on his wall and construct a 'why' that made him one of the most famous dancers and screen actors in history?

Walt Disney – a man renowned worldwide for his vivid and creative mind – was once fired by a newspaper editor for lack of ideas! He also went bankrupt several times before opening Disneyland. Walt never gave up – despite every obstacle and set back, he simply saw it as one more lesson taking him forward towards his ultimate success.

When life deals you a lemon, try something new and make lemonade.

No matter whether you have experienced awful things in life or not, there is an innate drive in every human to seek meaning and purpose. If we understand our 'why' then we can deal with any 'how' that life brings our way. Even in the darkest of nights, we can all find a way to let the light of who we really are shine through, if we believe in our hearts that there is a grander purpose. In the words of Frankl himself, *'what is to give light must endure burning'*.

If we can learn to interpret those events in ways that make sense, support and empower us, then I believe we can navigate any storm. I know that what happened to me was horrendous, but it was not half as debilitating as what I initially told myself it meant about me as a person and my future. It took me years to realise that I had made my mother's death mean I was defective in some way. However, I am the only one who can attribute meaning to the events in my life and the same is true for you.

Positive, negative or neutral – the choice is always yours. If you are not happy with the choices you have made so far in life the great news is that you can choose new meanings immediately that will drive you towards your bright and compelling future.

Don't make the same mistake I made – it's never too late to become the person you were meant to be!

How to incorporate this wisdom into your life

I've always loved reading the cartoons in newspapers. I love how they will take some event that's happening in the world and add a caption that changes it completely. The cartoon is as funny as the caption that was assigned to it ...

Often I will try and think of different ones and see if I could make them funnier. And it struck me one day that life really is much the same. The events and experiences are the cartoon and your beliefs about them become your caption.

Thinking back on my experience, I know that the captions I created about what my mother's death meant and what it meant for me as a person were wrong. And yet I allowed other people to put captions on my life. Not any more.

Whenever something happens to you that has the capacity to shrink your spirit, let your imagination recreate it as a cartoon and add a silly caption that makes you laugh out loud. As soon as you do, all the negative energy it holds will dissipate. Try it today!

Chapter 14

The very difficulty of a problem evokes abilities or talents which would otherwise, in happy times, never emerge to shine. ~ Horace

> Quintus Horatius Flaccus (or Horace to his friends) was a Roman lyric poet in the time of Augustus. He is the man responsible for the phrase 'carpe diem' – seize the day.

It is only when we are stretched that we discover new things about ourselves. Often it is adversity that allows us to become aware of and uncover our own innate talents.

One of the ideas often touted in the personal development industry is that you can do anything if you really want it badly enough. But is that really true?

I believe we all have the capacity for greatness, but not in everything. And why would we all want to be the same anyway? You need to identify and focus on the unique one or two skills that you have, that really make you stand out from the crowd, and concentrate on them exclusively.

I remember hearing Kieran Perkins speak at a Freedom Fox seminar I attended in February 2007. Because I didn't grow up in Australia, I don't think I had a true appreciation for the magnitude of his athletic accomplishments or the depth of his character. I was excited to hear him speak but I was not prepared for how much his presentation would touch my heart and inspire me. He is an absolute legendary sportsman, an admirable role model and a truly remarkable person. I consider it an honour and a privilege to have been in the audience that day.

For readers outside Australia the name may not be immediately recognisable, but Kieran Perkins is one of Australia's greatest swimmers and one of the world's best-ever long distance swimmers. He won two Olympic Gold medals in 1992 and 1996 in the 1500 metre freestyle and a silver medal in 2000. Perhaps his most famous victory was in the 1996 Atlanta Olympics … he had been out of form for some time and it was expected that fellow Australian Daniel Kowalski would beat him. Kieran qualified for the final by a mere 0.24 seconds, which meant he swam in lane 8, the hardest lane. To top it off he was suffering from a throat infection. Despite feeling unwell, Perkins gave the performance of his life to win gold in the race that stopped the nation. In his career he broke 12 world records and became the first person to hold Olympic, World, Commonwealth and Pan-Pacific titles simultaneously.

Kieran spent much of his allotted speaking time focusing on a very important concept – finding 'your' event. He wasn't born knowing that he would be a champion swimmer. Like other kids, he tried many sports – AFL, track and field, and cricket – and he just wasn't really all that good at any of them. Swimming was simply something he happened into. In fact, he originally began swimming as a rehabilitation exercise for a serious leg injury he incurred after running through a plate glass window. He learned the key strokes and techniques and tried various distances before he discovered that he was actually an excellent distance swimmer. He had finally found his niche and the rest is history.

Kieran stumbled upon his event literally by accident. If he hadn't been seriously injured running through a window, he may never have found his niche. Some would say it was a coincidence but he doesn't believe in mere coincidence – he believes that everyone has their unique talents, gifts or skills that make them stand out from the crowd. Interestingly, it is often in times of adversity that we have the opportunity to wander into uncharted territory and find those talents.

Many years ago, when I was in my early 20s, I took part in a four-day, 200 kilometre bike trip in Kananaskis country, which is in the heart of the Rocky Mountains. I was one of only two women on that trip and I was highly inexperienced – sort of a fair weather, city cyclist. The rest of our group were men that had significant cycling experience – both on and off road. I was very content to just sit back, enjoy the scenery and let the guys navigate the expedition.

The trip was marred by bad weather, mechanical failures, physical injuries and even a close encounter with a rather large brown bear that looked equally surprised to see us. Each day brought a new adventure and I was amazed at how well we all worked together to deal with the obstacles. On the last day, however, we ran into a fairly significant snag. We had managed to get off the trail somehow (it was very early in the Spring that year, the trail was not marked and it had not been travelled extensively yet). We must have pedalled for three or four hours before we collectively recognised that we were lost and that we only had a few hours of sunlight left. We had exhausted most of our water and food supply and we were unsure if we should stop for the night and set up camp or attempt to push on and find our way back to where we had dropped off the vehicles four days earlier.

Up until that point, I had been very content to just follow and go with the flow. The lack of sleep, the fear of not having enough supplies and the apprehension we all felt around being lost started to take its toll. I sensed the uneasiness even among the guys and they were starting to snap at each other. No one seemed to have a clear head and everyone had a different opinion on which way we needed to go in order to get us out of the bind that we were in. We had a map – but we had gone so far of course that we were not even exactly sure where we were in relation to any landmarks.

Strangely enough, I seemed to have a really strong intuition about where we where and where we needed to go. I have no idea why, but the terrain seemed strangely familiar to me. It took me quite a while to convince the guys that we need to backtrack a couple of kilometres to get to where I thought we had deviated from the trail. I had no real history of navigating anywhere with a map and I know the guys were very sceptical about following my gut instinct. At that point, we had really run out of choices, though and we had to do something fast. Thankfully, my presentiment paid off and we did in fact find our way back to the trail just before the sun went down. It still took us several hours to ride back to the vehicles but frankly we were all just happy to have made it.

To this day, I have no idea how I was able to navigate our way out of that predicament. To be honest, if we hadn't have gotten lost and stumbled into uncharted territory I am not entirely sure that I would have bothered paying attention to where we were. I only know that in a moment of adversity I uncovered a skill that I never knew I possessed. Strangely enough, I have travelled to many destinations around the world and always seemed to have an uncanny ability to find my way around.

Like Kieran, I'd uncovered a latent ability by accident and it's served me well ever since.

Did you know ... ?

In 1983 Dr Howard Gardner, professor of education at Harvard University, developed the theory of multiple intelligences. He suggested that measuring intelligence based on IQ was far too limited. Instead Dr Gardner proposes eight different intelligences to account for the broad range of human potential in children and adults:

- o Linguistic intelligence ('Word smart')
- o Logical-mathematical intelligence ('Number/reasoning smart')
- o Spatial intelligence ('Picture smart')
- o Bodily-kinesthetic intelligence ('Body smart')
- o Musical intelligence ('Music smart')
- o Interpersonal intelligence ('People smart')
- o Intrapersonal intelligence ('Self smart')
- o Naturalist intelligence ('Nature smart')

I remember reading about a study into these intelligences where young children were taught in a way that encouraged a range of different skills. The studies were looking to see if children demonstrated innate skills in a range of areas. In a normal schooling environment where the focus is placed on reading, writing and maths, these skills would not often be noticed and certainly not fostered. The study showed quite clearly that we all do have innate differences, that if known, could be very valuable in later life. For example, there was one little girl who seemed particularly capable of predicting who would make friends in the class. She was 'people smart' and was able to put people together that worked well together and enjoyed each other's company. Those skills are incredibly useful for, say, a recruitment consultant or a dating agency owner!

The other thing that Kieran said that day that affected me deeply was *'nobody ever achieves anything great without help'*. He spoke with extreme pride, gratitude and respect for the role that his wife and family played in his sporting career and achievements. That comment resonated very deeply with me – it was at that very moment that I penned the title of this book, On the Shoulders of Giants, and a brief outline for several chapters – as I sat in that audience and listened to the rest of his presentation. In many ways I owe this book to his inspirational words of wisdom and thought-provoking encouragement.

Perhaps adversity is the universe's way of helping us uncover our unique talents and abilities. We are all unique and we bring very different ideas and skills to the table. Expanding your experiences and trying new things is a great way to help you find those few skills that set you apart from everyone else. As Benjamin Disraeli said, *'There is no education like adversity'*.

How to incorporate this wisdom into your life

Like the little girl in the Harvard study it's likely that unless someone noticed these little quirks in your character, you may now be oblivious to them. The nuances or glimpses of your particular talent may now be lost to you as an adult.

One way to rediscover these parts of your nature is through psychometric testing. There are many to choose from but some of the best are Instinctive Drive (ID System), DISC and MBTI.

Instinctive Drive, as the name would suggest, is a tool to identify what you are instinctively driven toward. This shows us what our innate talents and vulnerabilities are and is a great tool for self-discovery. After answering a short questionnaire you are assigned a four-number code that relates to various drives. These drives include Verify, Authenticate, Complete and Improvise and indicate your innate operating system, which can help you work out how to get the best from yourself and others. People are different and ID celebrates that difference without pigeonholing you into a convenient box. Instead it offers strategies and ideas on how to work with your natural abilities and navigate the less helpful parts of your nature. ID is focused on the 'why' behind your actions and as such is a very powerful tool.

MBTI or Myers Briggs Type Indicator is more focused on the 'how'. MBTI looks at the behaviours and how best we work together based on personality characteristics. MBTI looks specifically at how we look at the world, make decisions and organise activities.

DISC is more focused on behavioural styles and preferences and can be useful in the field of leadership. The DISC Personality behavioural model looks at one's behaviour based on a four-dimensional model – the four quadrants assist you to determine your profile (which invariably includes a combination of the four styles), gives you insights into the behaviour of yourself and others and allows you to improve your interpersonal relationships and communication. The four quadrants are:

Dominance: These people tend to be direct, decisive, independent and results driven. They are strong-willed people who enjoy challenges and taking action. Their focus tends to be on the bottom line and results.

Influence: These individuals tend to be very social, optimistic and outgoing. They prefer participating on teams, sharing thoughts, and entertaining/energising others.

Steadiness: These people tend to be your team players and are supportive, stable, cooperative and helpful to others. They prefer being behind the scene and dislike change (prefer working in consistent and predictable ways). They are often good listeners and avoid change and conflict.

Conscientiousness: These people are often cautious and focused on details. They plan ahead, constantly check for accuracy/quality, and want to know 'how' and 'why'.

Chapter 15

Imagination is more important than knowledge. For knowledge is limited to all we now know and understand, while imagination embraces the entire world, and all there ever will be to know and understand. ~ Albert Einstein

Einstein was a German-born theoretical physicist. He is best known for his theory of relativity, his equation $E = mc2$. His contribution to science and philosophy cannot be under estimated. Einstein spent the last part of his life dedicated to finding a unified field theory. Einstein felt sure there must be one theory that would unite the known laws of physics such as relativity and gravity with the confusing world of quantum physics. His fellow scientists felt it was a wasted pursuit and yet we are now closer than ever to finding such a theory.

If you were to look around you right now, wherever you may be, you will see that almost everything in the world started first in the imagination. The chair that you are sitting on, the TV you watch in the evenings, the appliances you cook dinner on, the car you drive to work – everything first appeared as a thought in someone's mind. A passing notion that gathered momentum (and others!) to its cause until it became a reality.

Einstein reminds us that imagination is more important than knowledge. We grow up with ideas and beliefs about what is true and possible based on what someone else has told us. We accept what is delivered to us as knowledge without ever questioning its validity or authenticity. It becomes a way that we define who we are and what we are capable of. And in that respect it can be limiting. Francis Bacon famously said *'knowledge is power'* but that power isn't always positive!

If you consider the 'knowledge' that is given to people in a cult, it's quite clear that you can alter someone's reality based on the information you make available. There was a recent TV documentary called Strong City about a cult in New Mexico. The leader is a very charismatic individual who has structured a society to serve his own needs at the expense of everyone else. He had predicted the end of the world on a number of occasions, including the 31 October 2007. Each time the date passed without a catastrophic occurrence, he would simply set a new date. No one in the group thought it odd or questioned that his predictions never came true because he was at all times in control of the knowledge and the meaning ascribed to it and could bend and shape it to suit his own purposes. After all, he is a self-professed God and he controls what his followers believe, think and do. He could and did make his word the only 'truth'. And he had the entire colony believing that it was God's will that he (at 67) should have sex with virgin girls and even his son's own wife. Coincidentally, the latest date scheduled for the end of the world was 15 December 2007. Unsurprisingly, it passed without incident.

Much the same phenomenon can be witnessed around the world, through the calculated use and manipulation of the global media. How much of what we see in the news is true? How much is skewed to meet the requirements of certain political affiliations or agendas?

Any way you look at it, knowledge is power – and that power can be used for good or for evil. If you use it to constantly learn, challenge, create and expand your perspective, it can set you free. If you use it to lock down a viewpoint, constrain perspective and curtail exploration, you can imprison a nation.

Imagination, on the other hand, is limitless – what we deem possible or impossible is not bound by the constraints of our capabilities but rather by the clarity of the picture that we see in our mind's eye. The bigger and brighter the picture, the bigger we become to achieve it. Said another way, the more you demand of life, the more resources you will uncover to make it happen.

The imagination itself has no limits – perhaps that is why so many people are afraid to use it. It is easier to be satisfied and comfortable with what we have, even if it isn't what we want – better the devil we know.

To try and understand a little more about why imagination is so important it's worth looking at *Maslow's Hierarchy of Needs*. This was developed by Abraham Maslow in 1943.

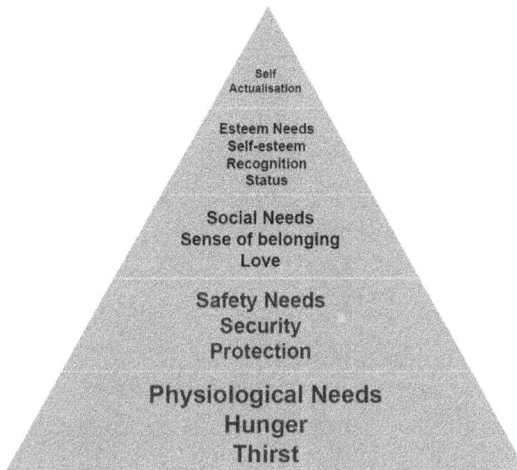

Self
Actualisation

Esteem Needs
Self-esteem
Recognition
Status

Social Needs
Sense of belonging
Love

Safety Needs
Security
Protection

Physiological Needs
Hunger
Thirst

Maslow proposed that we have certain needs that we seek to meet. Subsequent studies have expanded on this work and we will talk about Anthony Robbins' interpretation in a later chapter. At the very simplest level, we have physiological needs, the basic needs to eat and drink to keep us alive. After those needs, we crave safety and protection. After that, we need to feel a sense of belonging and certainty and it is this force that often keeps people in bad relationships or abusive situations. The need to belong to something – even something toxic, is strong. For some, the certainty of a bad relationship can seem comforting!

The next level is the need for recognition, which can be contrary to a sense of belonging. This is the human drive to stand out and be recognised for your contribution. We want to achieve great things and follow our dreams but we don't want to fail or look stupid. The drive to belong and stand out means that we are often looking for guarantees before we stick our head above the parapet! But there are no guarantees in life and the quality of your life is directly proportionate to the amount of uncertainty that you can comfortably handle.

Significance and recognition is the domain of the imagination – the dream that you have of who you were really meant to be. But a dream is not something that you wake up from – but something that wakes you up!

Just watch any small child, they haven't forgotten their true potential yet and are still full of imagination about what they will become. A child does not understand the concept of possible or impossible. It is only when we become much older and 'wiser' that we become imprisoned by artificial boundaries that serve to give us a sense of certainty and control but with that very little significance or recognition.

Regardless of how old you are, that child within us all still exists. He or she still has the hopes and dreams that you saw so clearly when you were only five or six. When I was around that age, there were so many things I wanted to be and do – a ballerina, Olympic champion figure skater, doctor, lawyer, mother, teacher, world traveller, writer and professional cat petter!

Even then, I knew that I wanted to really make a difference, to travel and share stories and to really connect with people on a deeper level but I had no idea how that dream or vision would play out in my life. I have had several careers – many of which challenged me intellectually and provided me with the opportunity to make a successful living and see the world. I always felt that I was capable of more – that I had the enthusiasm, passion and an obligation to share my unique experiences and inspire others to follow their hearts.

George Bernard Shaw once said, *'Some men look at things the way they are and ask why? I dream of things that are not and ask why not?'* To me, this is what imagination is all about.

When Walt Disney first imagined his little mouse no one could have predicted the outcome. Disney's dreams spawned an industry that has seen special effects advance at an extraordinary pace. The open landscape of Disney's imagination created theme parks around the world that have brought joy to millions of families. As Einstein said, *'Imagination is everything. It is the preview of life's coming attractions'.* Einstein even developed the theory of relativity by running what he called a thought experiment. He imaged himself riding on the end of a light beam. By using his imagination to consider what it would be like to ride a light beam, which of course is impossible in 'real life', he was able to gain a new understanding that led to the theory of relativity.

Imagination is limitless and is possessed in equal measure by everyone. You don't need a college education to use your imagination; the lack of money doesn't hinder your use of imagination nor does your social circumstance or environmental conditions. Like a butterfly emerging from a cocoon, imagination allows you to stretch your wings and really see what's possible. Combine that with an insatiable thirst for knowledge and new information and you will be truly astonished at what you are capable of.

Did you know ... ?

Psycho-Cybernetics is a classic personal development book published in 1960 by Dr Maxwell Maltz and was based on 29 years worth of research. Most of the current speakers in the area of personal development, including Zig Ziglar, Tony Robbins, Brian Tracy and others owe a significant debt to Maxwell Maltz. No other approach to self-improvement has ever come close to reaching 30 million people with almost no advertising or promotion.

Dr Maltz was a cosmetic plastic surgeon who operated on over 25,000 people in his career. He healed a lot of people with his scalpel – but some of the people he operated on didn't notice a difference in their appearance, even though he had turned their disfigured faces into works of art. He recognised that, in addition to the reconstruction work on the outside, the patient needed to have reconstruction work on the 'inside'. It was clear that people did not see what was there. They saw what their imagination told them was there. Maltz believed that the imagination played a far bigger role in our lives that we realise. He said that creative imagination was not the reserve of poets, philosophers and inventors but that all human beings act, feel and perform in accordance with what they imagine to be true about themselves and their environment.

This basic law of mind is no more graphically demonstrated than in a hypnotised subject. If the subject is told they are at the North Pole they will not only shiver and appear to look cold but they will also develop goose pimples and feel a drop in temperature. Tell a hypnotised subject that their finger is touching is a red-hot poker and he or she will not only grimace with pain but their cardiovascular and lymphatic systems will react just as if the finger was touching a red-hot poker. Inflammation and perhaps even blisters could appear on the skin. That's the work of the imagination and nothing more!

How to incorporate this wisdom into your life

Muhammad Ali said, *'The man who has no imagination has no wings.'* So give your imagination room to fly and answer the following question …

'If money was no object and I could not fail, what would I do with my life?'

Write down five things. For each one take a few moments and imagine what that would be like? Fully engage in the experience and revel in the possibility of that life. And remember most people overestimate what they can do in one year and seriously underestimate what they can do in ten. Take action toward at least one of these dreams today!

Chapter 16

We don't see things as they are, we see things as we are. ~ The Talmud

> The Talmud is a record of discussions regarding Jewish law, ethics, customs and history. The Talmud has two components, the Mishnah (c. 200 CE) which is the first written compendium of Judaism's Oral Law; and the Gemara (c. 500 CE), a discussion of the Mishnah and related Tannaitic writings that often ventures onto other subjects. These are sacred texts of significant significance to both the Jewish and broader community.

As a sacred text, the *Talmud* offers us a perspective into the past that is as relevant today as it was when it was written. The phrase above means that the world outside is not separate from the world inside. So much so that we do not see what is going on in the world as an objective bystander but as a co-creator.

How we perceive events or interpret actions is never based on 'truth', only personal truth. Say you wake up one morning and decide to open the mail before you leave for work. The first letter you open is your monthly credit card statement. This makes you really upset because you can't see how you're going to pay the mounting debts you are creating. In that frame of mind you begin the drive to work. Someone cuts you off at the traffic lights and that just adds fuel to the fire. During the course of the morning you have separate arguments with two colleagues.

Eventually after a 'terrible morning', you retreat to a favourite little café to try and wind down. When you do eventually relax you assume that everyone, including your work colleagues, must have gotten out of bed on the wrong side this morning.

But it had nothing to do with them. We do not see things as they are, we see things as we are. Because you were negative and frustrated you chose to interpret the various events from that perspective. For all you know the person who cut you off could have been in a desperate hurry to get to hospital because his wife was having a baby. You didn't notice that your work colleagues were doing their best and were acting no different than usual. What was different was you – you were angry and so you perceived and interpreted events and situations that fuelled your rage.

So often in life we think everything happens on the outside but most of life actually happens inside and we project that out into the world through our thoughts, words and actions. As a result we don't get what we want – we get who we are. If we dish out anger and resentment we will experience anger and resentment from others.

If we consider that we delete huge portions of the potential information that is available to us why do we choose to delete all the good stuff and leave just the anger, frustrations and limitations?

The truth of the *Talmud's* insight is often easier to see in someone else's life than our own. Perhaps you've been out with friends and you were talking about *Big Brother* and one of your friends said, 'I don't like John, he's just so arrogant.' Someone else might disagree and think that he's actually just shy and trying to cover it up. Another friend might have another completely different take on John. What strikes you is that every one of your friends noticed something in John that was actually a reflection of them. Your friend that noticed the arrogance does actually have a little of that in herself sometimes. The friend that didn't notice that doesn't have an arrogant bone in his body but he is unsure of himself in certain situations.

It's not possible to see something in someone that is not a part of you. And that means good and bad. If you are a generous person you notice generosity in others. If generosity is not a trait you have in abundance, then acts of generosity may pass by completely unnoticed.

For most of my adult life, I saw myself as a victim. I identified so strongly with all of the negative things that I have experienced, that I could not differentiate between me and the memory of what happened to me.

104

What I had been through became the essence of who I was and from that position of disempowerment, I literally attracted all sorts of events and individuals into my life to mirror back and validate the view that I had of myself.

This is why I feel that often victim support groups can do more harm than good. Shortly after my mother's death, I was invited to join a national Victims of Violence group that was founded by a couple that had tragically lost their son in 1992. The purpose of the group was to support each other and lobby the government for changes to penal codes and to support the grieving families of other murder victims.

And yet whenever we got together to help each other and discuss initiatives emotions were always running high. Everyone wanted to speak and no one wanted to listen. There was often talk of the death penalty and the need for the perpetrators of these atrocities to pay for their crimes. There was a lot of emphasis on the criminals and making them 'pay' and very little focus on what the survivors could do to reclaim their life, find peace and begin living again.

Please understand that I believe wholeheartedly that there has to be consequences for people who commit crimes but I do not believe that the death penalty is the answer – not for the victim, the criminal or the survivors. I do not believe that you can 'even the score' by taking another life and I would argue that no real 'closure' or peace comes from it. As Gandhi once said, *'An eye for an eye makes the whole world blind.'* He encouraged us to 'Hate the sin, love the sinner' and suggests that, *'The weak can never forgive. Forgiveness is the attribute of the strong.'*

I also do not believe that it would act as an effective deterrent. You can't stop war with war; you can't end violence with violence. It just doesn't work that way. We have to change the way we see the world and again as Gandhi points out, *'We have to become the change we want to see in the world.'* If we want to see less violence we have to be less violent. As hard as this may be to stomach (and believe me I've found it hard) the only way to change the nature of our world is to find forgiveness and add love to the equation. Directing your hate toward some outside source is only ever really damaging you. It may act as a perfect diversion that focuses your rage but sooner or later you will have to deal with the unfathomable terror, regret, shame, anger and grief – and *still* find a way to forgive and move on. That's not easy and I still struggle with that too but I know in my heart it's the only avenue for liberation.

Even though I was sitting in a room full of people at the victim support group, many of whom had experienced loss equal to or greater than mine, I never came away from a single meeting feeling supported, understood or at peace. In fact, I only felt more upset and agitated. Eventually, I simply stopped going. I was really torn between wanting to make a difference by affecting change through legislation and preserving my own sanity. In the end, I chose sanity and it was one of the best decisions that I have made as it put me on the path toward healing.

I met some of the nicest people in that group but the circumstances were such that it was impossible for anyone to heal. With that much pain, vengeance and fury in one room, it was not possible for any of us to see things as they really were, we only saw things as we were. And there were no positive, loving, long-term solutions from that vantage point.

Often our relationships or interactions with others provide us with a unique opportunity to see ourselves as others see us. I didn't want to remain a victim and I didn't want to stay in an environment where that's how I would be categorised. Becoming attached to that negative identity can be suicide and certainly wasn't helping me to find new perspectives so that I could find some peace and move on. And that's my biggest concern with victim support groups. I think they are extremely valuable in finding others that can truly understand your pain and offer a level of acceptance and support that perhaps others can't offer. But staying in that environment and re-hashing your pain over and over again is counter-productive. You have to use it as a springboard to help you regroup and get back into life, not as a place to wallow in mutual suffering.

This idea of attracting who we are is particularly crucial when it comes to finding a partner. Unsurprisingly I struggled with issues of abandonment for years and I just didn't feel good enough or worthy of love. It was therefore no revelation that I attracted prospective partners who were only too happy to oblige me in reinforcing this negative belief. None of them were bad men, they were just lost souls who didn't know who they were and didn't have much to give in a relationship. What I eventually realised is that I too was just a lost soul and I was attracting who I was, not who or what I wanted.

Dating is a process like any other and there is always an element of trial and error but when you keep meeting the same people over and over again, the only common denominator is you. We all meet incompatible potential partners and so we move on but to continue to do it time and again is a clear indication that something is not adding up – with you. We need relationships and other people not just because of the obvious reasons of companionship and support but because they offer us a unique opportunity to see ourselves as others see us and find ways to solve our own issues and become whole in our own right. We are never one half of a whole – we must be whole in ourselves in order to attract another whole person and live a whole life.

For me, I had to learn to love myself again first. The same can be true of millions of people around the world for a variety of reasons connected with their own experiences. It took me a long time to understand that I needed to *be* the sort of person that I wanted to marry. I was searching for all those qualities in someone else so I might have them by default. But I needed to embody those qualities myself, move away from the victim mentality and take control of my life again. And when I did, things changed.

Our external relationships are always a current reflection of our internal relationship with ourselves. It is a direct correlation to our own consciousness. It is one thing to sit down and write a goal to attract a partner with certain, specific qualities, attitudes, values and beliefs. But until you evolve yourself and become someone who lives by those specific qualities, attitudes, values and beliefs, you won't attract what you want. We attract what we are and that can be really hard to take when you first realise it.

If you want a great partner, be a great partner – it's as simple as that! Become the person you wish to attract and that person will be attracted to you.

The insights other people offer you are a chance for you to make changes in yourself so that you stop attracting the same people and events over

Did you know ... ?

Shakespeare hit the nail on the head when he said, 'Me *thinks he doth protest too much*.' Often those most vocal about a particular trait or personal characteristic are often the ones that possess that trait themselves. When someone gets very upset about something or someone else it's usually a pretty good indication they have just seen an unconscious replication of themselves and they don't like it!

I remember watching a TV show about a study of homosexuality. There were two groups of men tested. The first that didn't have any issue with homosexuality and another group that was very vocal about it being wrong. They were each hooked up to monitors and left in a room with gay reading and visual material. Those who had no feeling either way about homosexuality and felt it was an individual choice, didn't react to the material. Interestingly the monitors measuring the response of those that professed a strong aversion to homosexuality indicated that the material sexually stimulated many of them!

and over. Once we see our part in the drama – that distinction alone will break the pattern and new tomorrows are possible. As William M Thackeray said, *'The world is a looking glass and gives back to every man the reflection of his own face'*.

A word of caution before we leave this topic ... This is not an excuse to blame others. Often people with a little grasp of this idea can start using it as a justification for poor behaviour, 'Oh you're just upset because this is a mirror of you.' Say, for example, I behaved badly toward you and you got upset, there may very well be some part of my behaviour that seems unpleasantly familiar to you because you know in your heart you have been guilty of the same thing. Or maybe I just behaved badly and you are justifiably offended by my actions. Don't let others justify their inappropriate behaviour using this caveat. This concept offers us a chance to take responsibility for ourselves so we can heal; it is not a 'get out of jail free card!'

How to incorporate this wisdom into your life

When you get upset about someone or something it's a good indication that you've just unconsciously seen an aspect of yourself and you don't like it!

Next time you find yourself reacting above and beyond what you would consider to be usual for the situation, take a moment to assess what the other person has done. These are the times where 'the crime' doesn't in any way warrant your response. Maybe you can think of times where you have reacted to something and been embarrassed or shocked afterwards because you didn't understand the strength of your reaction. Perhaps someone borrowed something without asking? Perhaps someone damaged something precious to you and didn't show any remorse for their action. Ask yourself, 'Have I ever borrowed something without asking? Have I ever damaged someone else's precious possessions and not confessed or said sorry? Once you see the connection you will find yourself feeling surprisingly calm, you may even have a little chuckle to yourself. Whatever you feel new understanding emerges and you will be more forgiving this time and in the future – you have learned the lesson you were meant to learn. Make your apologies to the appropriate people, including yourself and move on.

Chapter 17

Don't practice until you get it right, practice until you can't get it wrong. ~ Anon

I have chosen this anonymous quote partly because it describes perfectly what I want to convey and partly because it is anonymous. Some of the giants in our life are people we never know. We are all connected and there is no way to really know everyone who has positively influenced our life. A passing comment from a stranger about your favourite shoes, a smile on a cold morning from someone on the train – these are all anonymous people who shape our experiences. Never underestimate the power you hold to make someone's day a little brighter ...

Considered the greatest diver of all time, Greg Louganis is a four-time world champion, four-time Pan American gold medallist and winner of two double gold medals for the United States at two consecutive Olympics.

Greg was a true champion – he had impeccable form, he was incredibly consistent and he was the first diver to ever receive perfect tens on a dive in international competition. But his path to success was far from easy – he is dyslexic and he struggled to read and write both before and after his career in the pool. When he retired he became active in theatre and dance but found following a script quite daunting. He, therefore, drew upon a visualisation process developed in his earliest childhood days.

Louganis says he used the memory of his mistakes – like hitting his head on the diving platform at the 1988 Olympics – to focus on preventing them. His technique didn't include 'imagining perfection' which is what many coaches advocate, but imagining his mistakes so he could find ways to correct them. In an interview he said *'I visualised what could go wrong, and how to make it right'*, a technique that's helped him on and off the diving board.

So often we are told to always expect the best and I've said as much in this book. But life isn't just about a positive attitude – it's about preparation, practise and hard work.

Life, like diving, is unpredictable. Rarely do we ever hit the 'sweet spot' on the board of life and enter the water in the perfect position to execute the move we have planned. More often than not, we stumble, slide and falter only to discover that we now have no choice but to make something out of it. As I have said before, sometimes you have to 'make chicken soup out of chicken shit'. It is often in these times of desperation that we accomplish our greatest feats. We find ourselves in a crisis situation and in that moment we stretch beyond the finite boundaries of probability and skill and into the realm of possibility and inspiration.

I started figure skating at age five and was involved at a competitive level in ladies singles, freestyle pairs and dance pairs over the course of my 13-year career. Even back in mid 1970s, a considerable amount of money was invested by the governing bodies on off-ice training and mental preparation, including creative visualisation. Around the time I was 11 or 12, the top skaters in each province were selected to attend intensive training sessions with top coaches from both the US and Canada. In addition to training with the best of the best (one of my peers, Kurt Browning, went on to be arguably the best male skaters that Canada has ever produced – four-time World and Canadian champion), we were exposed to training techniques, meditation and philosophies that were leading edge at the time.

Under the normal training regime, it was fairly common to warm up for ten to 15 minutes and then run through a freestyle program. Most of us would have been used to about two to three hours per day of freestyle or ice-dance practice on ice. Rarely would any of us have done extensive off-ice cardio, weights or modern dance on the same day as our on-ice practice.

It was quite a shock as an 11-year-old to be away from home in a strange city, subject to strong dietary scrutiny and exposed to eight hours a day of regimented training. I can still remember the first day – we ran, swam, did weight training and then had an entire hour of stretch class. By the time we actually got onto the ice it was late afternoon and I was already tired. Then the fun began: we were asked to perform our freestyle programs while the instructors watched and critiqued. It was unbelievable how many of us were simply unprepared.

The next day brought an entirely new surprise – we were asked to perform our freestyle programs with only a short one-minute warm up. Again, this exposed significant flaws and deficiencies in the preparation of most of us. Very few of the skaters could make it through programs containing double jumps, difficult combinations and complex footwork with only a one-minute warm up.

For me it was an invaluable experience – from the perspective of my skating career and also for life in general. Day by day, we were exposed to new ways of doing things and our skills and endurance were tested and stretched under unexpected conditions. We started to learn that it is simply not enough to show up, run through a session or two and call it a day. In order to be a champion, you literally had to be willing to do what the competition was unwilling to do – practise and practise until you simply could not get it wrong.

As I said earlier, I had the privilege of skating alongside one of the best male skaters of all time. Kurt Browning was technically an excellent skater – he possessed great skill, the right body type and he was an outstanding showman. I think he would have excelled under almost any circumstances. There were two other male skaters in our group who were technically more gifted, but who did not go on to win at the national or international level. So what made Kurt so special – why did he excel while others simply fizzled out?

What made him a champion was his incredible persistence and commitment to excellence. He excelled at all aspects – jumps, figures, spins, showmanship and footwork – not just at one or two. Kurt also didn't believe in half measures – he was one of the first kids on the ice and the last to leave at night. He took pride in everything that he did and he never tired of finding new ways to improve his skills and performance. His tenacity and versatility made an indelible impression on me. Doing things right is only half the puzzle. Understanding what constitutes 'wrong' so you can use those insights to make yourself strong is just as important.

Take Muhammad Ali for example. In perhaps the most anticipated boxing match of all time, Muhammad Ali met George Foreman who was eight years his junior. The clash was to take place in the central African nation of Zaire and became known as 'The Rumble in the Jungle'. Almost no one gave the former heavyweight champion a chance of winning. Foreman had knocked out both Joe Frazier and Ken Norton in the second round – whereas both of these opponents had given Ali some long and tough battles in the ring.

During the bout, Ali essentially re-invented himself. Leading up to the night, Ali boasted that he was going to float like a butterfly and use his speed to avoid and outbox Foreman – a tactic that everyone expected and had previously served him well. However, Ali shocked the fans and Foreman when he came out in Round 1 and began scoring with his explosive right hand lead. Foreman took nine powerful shots to the head in that round but remained on his feet. Ali then switched tactics again and spent the better part of rounds 2-7 on the ropes taking Foreman's heavy body shots and verbally taunting the younger boxer. Ali knew that Foreman had won 37 out of his 40 previous fights by knockout, mostly in the first three rounds, and he suspected that Foreman would simply not have the staying power to fight more than seven or eight long rounds.

Ali saw an opportunity to outlast Foreman and capitalised on it. By the end of the seventh round, Foreman was simply exhausted. In the eighth round, Ali came alive and countered with stinging straight punches to Foreman's head, which caused Foreman to hit the canvas. Ali's tactic of leaning on the ropes and absorbing body shots was later coined 'the rope a dope'. Still to this day it's considered a dangerous tactic and a sign of impending defeat – and proof that in the right hands, even the wrong tactics work!

Ali regained his heavyweight title at the age of 32 and went on to be named the athlete of the Century by *QC Magazine* and Sportsman of the Century by *Sports Illustrated*.

He was an amazing athlete and an astute strategist. He knew that Foreman had him beat in the categories of size, speed and skill. However, he understood the strengths and limitations of his own ability and he applied them to his best advantage so he could win. Arguably, the better 'boxer' did not win on the day. However, few can argue with the fact that Ali won fair and square and he proved to the world that when you have the will of a champion, you can surmount even the stiffest odds.

Did you know ... ?

Nicknamed 'The Great One,' ice hockey player Wayne Gretzky was called 'the greatest player of all time'. He set 40 regular-season records, 15 playoff records, six All-Star records, won four Stanley Cups with the Edmonton Oilers, and won nine MVP awards and ten scoring titles. He is the only player ever to total over 200 points in a season – a feat he accomplished four times in his career. Gretzky's dominance throughout his career was attributed to the amount of time he practiced. He was also considered by many to be a natural prodigy in the sport – he had a good shot, moved the puck very well, never quit, and played both defence as well as offence.

In terms of basic athletic abilities, Gretzky was not impressive. He was six feet tall, weighing only 160 pounds as an 18-year-old rookie in 1979. At the beginning of Gretzky's NHL career, many critics at the time opined that Gretzky was 'too small, too wiry, and too slow to be a force in the NHL'. On the other hand, he had no rival in his intelligence and reading of the game, being able to anticipate where the puck was going to be and execute the right move at the right time. He is famous for saying, 'I skate to where the puck is going to be, not where it is.'

How to incorporate this wisdom into your life

Planning for what you want is only ever part of the solution. If you are to make a presentation at work then it makes sense to be well prepared. It is wise to run through the presentation in front of a variety of people so you can get feedback and see where your weak spots are. But you might also want to consider all the things that could go wrong. And make plans to circumvent those issues. Run through the worst possible questions that you could be asked so that you have answers ready, should they come up.

You will be so prepared for all eventualities that the extra confidence you feel will by default improve your performance. Why? Because you practised and prepared until you can't get it wrong.

Chapter 18

If you follow your bliss, doors will open for you that wouldn't have opened for anyone else. ~ Joseph Campbell

Joseph Campbell was a lifelong student and teacher on the human spirit and mythology. His fundamental belief was that all spirituality is a search for some elemental force that is 'unknowable' because it exists before words and knowledge. Metaphor through myth is therefore a powerful way for us to understand something that is in many ways unknowable. According to Campbell the religions of the world were just various masks to the same basic transcendental truth. He died in 1987 after a short battle with cancer but was one of the few serious thinkers ever to be embraced by popular culture.

In interviews about his book *The Power of Myth* with Bill Moyers, recorded shortly before his death, Campbell said that, *'if you follow your bliss you put yourself on a kind of track that has been there all the while, waiting for you, and the life that you ought to be living is the one you are living'*.

Since then the catch cry – follow your bliss – has been hijacked by the personal development movement. It had been used as a caveat to justify all sorts of pointless pursuits of self-indulgence.

But that was not what Campbell was saying. He was always keen to point out that following your bliss was not about doing whatever you liked whenever you wanted to. It was about identifying the pursuit that you were most passionate about and giving yourself to that absolutely.

When you are able to do that, you are in a position to fulfil your highest potential and serve humanity.

In Sanskrit, which is the great spiritual language of the world, there are three terms that represent the brink or jumping-off point into the ocean of transcendence: sat-chit-ananda. 'Sat,' means being, 'Chit' means consciousness and 'Ananda' means bliss or rapture. Campbell said, *'I don't know whether my consciousness is proper consciousness or not; I don't know whether what I know of my being is my proper being or not; but I do know where my rapture is. So let me hang on to rapture, and that will bring me both my consciousness and my being'.* Considering the incredible contribution he made to his field, it looks like his theory is one that worked in his own life.

This idea of bliss in many ways is as logical as it is mystical. If we are passionate about something, that something becomes one of our dominating thoughts and it is biologically programmed to appear on our internal radar. As a result, our brain ensures that anything in connection to that passion is consciously noted by our mind.

I think everyone experiences this notion of bliss in different aspects of their lives and at different times. For me, my earliest recollection of this connection to bliss dates back to the times that I spent with my maternal grandmother in her kitchen and in the garden when I was three or four years old. We were inseparable in those days – my grandmother cared for me during the day while both my parents were at work and I literally spent the day watching and copying everything that she did. She was an incredible cook – everything was prepared from scratch with fresh ingredients and grandma's magical touch.

She used to bake pies and make perogies in the kitchen while I watched attentively. She always gave me my own dough and I would roll it out for hours on the table with my little rolling pin, covered in flour up to my ears. She would make homemade jam, tomato juice, cabbage rolls, beetroot, dill pickles and so many other things that we now buy pre-packaged from the grocery store. They may be more convenient now but they certainly don't taste as good as hers.

In the summer, I would often sit for hours in the garden on a tiny, white wooden chair. My grandmother would pick baby peas, carrots, radishes and tomatoes out of the garden and wash them for me with the hose on the side of the garage. I would sit there for hours eating my veggies, watching the birds and butterflies and talking with my grandma as she weeded and watered the garden and tended to all of her flowers. It was quality time – I felt a strong bond with her and a real appreciation for her passion for growing things, cooking and taking care of others.

I am by no means a professional chef or gardener but I have always had a natural ability and a flair for pulling things together in the kitchen. Like her, I just have a feel for what goes together and I rarely feel the need to measure or consult a traditional cookbook. For me, cooking for others is a real privilege and just something that I am very passionate about. When I am in the zone in my kitchen, preparing to cook a meal for guests, I feel so connected to the same state of bliss I had when I was a young child in my grandmother's kitchen.

Over the years, I have been lucky enough to experience that same state of bliss many times – performing Swan Lake with some of the principal dancers from the Royal Winnipeg ballet company, teaching a child to skate, volunteering to organise a charity telethon, starting my own business, decorating, creating crafts and moving to Australia.

Following your bliss is more than just about pursuing a profession that suits your personality and allows you to achieve your highest potential. I think it is broader than that. For me, it's about doing what I feel compelled to do in my heart – and that extends to every aspect of my life.

At the time I decided to move to Australia, it truly was a leap of faith. I did not yet have a job, home, or a support network established in that country. Yet somehow, I felt a real passion to follow my bliss and pursue a new start. I had previously been there on a holiday and felt an instant affinity and connection to the country and the people. I felt that I was destined to live in Melbourne – it just felt right.

I moved within about nine days of making my decision and everything fell into place very quickly after I landed. Doors opened and opportunities came up for me that simply would not have existed had I stayed in Canada. I was surprisingly calm and confident about everything – the job, friends and a place to live quickly fell into place one after the other effortlessly and easily.

Looking back on it now, even I am amazed at the fact that everything unfolded so perfectly and fluidly. There were an infinite number of things that could have gone wrong and so many ways my journey could have been thwarted had it not been for the fact that I trusted my gut and followed my bliss. Even though I am getting better and better at trusting my own inner knowing with practice, I admit that I still struggle with it from time to time. It is easy to get caught up in worrying about all the things that could go wrong – looking for all the outside assurances, 'signs' and guarantees that everything will work out. In the words of the great poet David Whytem *'Sometimes everything has to be inscribed across the heavens so you can find the one line already written inside you'.*

This experience and many others have taught me that I am always exactly where I am supposed to be. I have a deeper appreciation and respect for the wisdom of my own intuition and I have learned that it is actually easier to connect to my own inner voice than to look for and consult 100 external opinions. Looking back, I cannot think of a single time where my intuition has led me astray – more often than not, I have tended to get myself into trouble when I deliberately went against my immediate instinct.

Only you can find your true path. The answers are already inside you. More than likely those answers have been trying to get your attention for years. Do not make the mistake of looking to others for they can only share their truth based on what they have tried and failed to do in their own life. Plus, once you really connect to and follow your bliss, doors will open and opportunities will present themselves that simply would not have appeared for anyone else.

Did you know ... ?

Joseph Campbell also believed in the power of coincidence as a way to point the direction of your bliss and validate when you are where you are meant to be. He once told the following story at a seminar he was presenting at the Esalen Institute:

'We happen to live in New York City, on the fourteenth floor in an apartment on Waverly Place and Sixth Avenue. The last thing you would expect to see in New York City is a praying mantis. The praying mantis plays the role of the hero in the Bushman folklore. I was reading the Bushman mythology – all about the praying mantis. The room in which I was doing this reading has two windows; one window faces up Sixth Avenue, the other window faces toward the Hudson River. This is the window I look out of all the time: the window on the Sixth Avenue, I do not think I have opened more than twice during the forty-odd years we have lived there.

'I was reading about the praying mantis – the hero – and suddenly I felt an impulse to open the window facing Sixth Avenue. I opened the window and looked out to the right and there was a praying mantis walking up the building. He was there, right on the rim of my window! He was this big [showing the size]; he looked at me and his face looked just like a Bushman's face. This gave me the creeps! You might say this was a coincidence, but what are the odds for something like this to happen by chance?'

Perhaps coincidences are the universes way of patting you on the back and saying, 'good job, you're on the right track'? Perhaps they are the cosmic indicators of being on the right path and following your bliss.

How to incorporate this wisdom into your life

Have you ever had the experience of working on something and completely losing track of time? Hours pass like minutes and you find that you are totally immersed in what you are doing. This state is often referred to as 'flow' and is a good indication that you have found your bliss.

Think of the experiences in your life and write down five times were you have lost track of time. Assess all of the situations and find out what common characteristics are present in each situation. Being consciously aware of these moments will allow you to find the common denominator in each so that you can better uncover your bliss. Bliss doesn't have to be something like painting or writing or some activity it can just as easily be a way of working. It may involve thinking time or time to interact with others.

Chapter 19

Your limitations and success will be based, most often, on your own expectations for yourself. Expect the best, plan for the worst and prepare to be surprised. ~ Denis Waitley

Denis Waitley is one of America's most respected authors and speakers on high performance human achievement. With over 10 million audio programs sold in 14 languages, Denis Waitley is one of the most listened-to voices on personal and career success. He is the author of 15 non-fiction books, including several international best sellers, 'Seeds of Greatness', 'Being the Best', 'The Winner's Edge', 'The Joy of Working' and 'Empires of the Mind'. Waitley is a graduate of the US Naval Academy at Annapolis, a former Navy pilot and he holds a doctorate degree in human behaviour.

Our thoughts, values, beliefs and attitudes all play out through our expectations. Collectively those expectations exert a huge influence on our results. For example, if you go for a job interview but you don't expect to get the job, everything about you on that day will conspire to deliver that outcome. If you don't expect to get the job, you won't make sure that you arrive on time. If you don't expect to get it you won't take that extra care in your appearance. If you don't expect to get the job then you won't focus on the interview and put your best foot forward. You won't be genuinely enthusiastic about the position and your lack of passion will come through. You won't feel it worthwhile to research the position or the company so as to really know what they are looking for. You won't think to ask questions and truly engage in the two way process. Now I'm not saying that if you confidently expect to get the job that you will always get the job but I am saying that if you confidently expect not to get the job, there is no way on earth you will be proven wrong!

Often our expectations for ourselves are tempered by earlier defeats. It is difficult to fail and to get back up and try again. It becomes easier not to give everything your best shot – then at least you can shrug it off and remind yourself that you didn't really want it anyway! Right?

But the only person you're selling out is you.

Did you know ... ?

Richard Bach once said, 'In order to win, you must expect to win'. And he should know! Richard Bach is an American writer most famous for his massive 1970's bestseller *Jonathan Livingstone Seagull*. Although it contains less than 10,000 words, it broke all hardcover sales records since *Gone with the Wind* and has gone on to sell over 30 million copies. A feat made all the more remarkable because Jonathan Livingstone Seagull was rejected by 26 publishers. Bach never gave up he always expected that one day he'd find a publisher who would share his enthusiasm for his book. At number 27, he found Macmillan Publishing and they said, 'Yes'.

Robert Fulgrum wrote a very clever little book that became a New York Times Bestseller called, *All I Really Needed to Know, I Learned in Kindergarten*. In it he details simple yet poignant anecdotes about living and the significance that can be found in even the smallest of details. I second Robert's notion about expectations and the elemental truths we learn at kindergarten. The lessons may sound simple but the implications for life are truly profound. Lessons like – don't hit people, clean up your own mess, say sorry when you hurt somebody, don't hide too well – it's good to be found.

In many ways, school is a microcosm for life. I feel fortunate because I always did pretty well in school. Apart from anything else it represented a safe place for me, somewhere I felt at ease, stimulated and competent. However, by the time I reached Grade 7 things started to unravel. I had just entered junior high school and my parents were in the throes of a very ugly divorce. My body was doing what young bodies do and my hormones were on a rollercoaster ride. It was a recipe for disaster. I remember needing a lot more attention than I was getting and I felt very frustrated and confused about all the changes in my life. Naturally my internal chaos attracted external chaos in the guise of new friends who were experiencing challenges and issues of their own.

Thankfully, we were basically good kids, just a bit mischievous. I remember one day I came across the answers to the entire year's science tests in the lab area. I copied them and passed along the questions and answers to about eight of my closest classmates. Suffice to say, that many of us did quite well in science that semester!

Eventually either the teachers caught on to us or someone reported us to the principal. I distinctly remember my English teacher Mr Sept asking me to step outside into the hallway with him the next day. I was expecting to get an earful – Mr Sept was one of the toughest and most intimidating teachers in school. He was not a man who gave praise lightly. A student had to earn his respect. I cared very much what he thought – I always put my best effort into my submissions for his class and I hung on every word of feedback that he gave me.

The American actress Patricia Neal once said, *'A master can tell you what he expects of you. A teacher, though, awakens your own expectations'*. Mr Sept was that teacher for me.

When he took me out into the hallway, he did something that completely took me by surprise. Instead of berating or shaming me, he opened the door for me to really tell him what was going on in my life. He told me that I had earned the highest mark in each of the core subjects for all students in Grade 7. He knew that I didn't need the answers to any test in any subject and he wanted to know why I did it. Regardless of what I had to say, he already knew the answer – or at least I suspected by his reaction that he did. I don't think he was one bit surprised when I broke down and cried and told him that I just wanted the other kids to like me and that I wanted my parents to get back together again.

Mr Sept said something to me that day that I will remember for the rest of my life. He said, *'I think that you can be anything you set your mind to and I am very proud of you for what you have already accomplished'*.

To this day, I do not know if he completely understood what was really going on in my life. I am not entirely sure if he comprehended the magnitude of the gift that he gave me that day. I remember it like it was yesterday and it affected me in the most profound way. Despite my behaviour, he showed me nothing but unconditional support. It was a new experience for me in many ways as it often felt as if my parents' support and love was conditional on my performance. Both my parents expected me to do well and were deeply disappointed when I didn't perform. In fact I soon discovered that the only way to get their attention about anything was to screw up – especially in the middle of their divorce!

With Mr Sept's continued encouragement and belief in me I was able to re-establish a spark of belief I had in myself, albeit a little dampened by my circumstances. I developed a real love and curiosity for reading and writing. I have no doubt that this newfound passion and enthusiasm affected my academic performance throughout my schooling and onto my ultimate career choices.

I didn't see him much after I completed Grade 7. I grew up and moved away from the small town and got busy living my life. The next time I saw him was during the week I returned to my home town for two funerals – my mother's and my best friends' brother. Mr Sept wasn't teaching any longer, he was working at a funeral home. When I attended the second funeral that week, Mr Sept was there. We talked briefly and he expressed his condolences. I told him that I had just completed law school and that I had gotten an internship at the top law firm in the city. Mr Sept just looked at me and said, *'I'm not surprised, I knew you could do anything that you set your mind to.'*

Sometimes in life we encounter teachers and friends who do not set the bar very high for our academic pursuits or our futures. Mr Sept did the exact opposite for me. He set the bar so high that I felt obligated to apply myself to live up to his expectations. And in doing so he taught me one of the most important lessons of my life that our limitations and success are based on our own expectations for our self.

There is little to be gained by comparing yourself to those around you. The only real measure of your success is how you fair against your own personal best. Learning to expect the best from yourself and demanding that continuous improvement can have dramatic effects on your long-term destination. If we are constantly asking more of ourselves, making small incremental shifts in our thinking, expectations and therefore our results, then we can make massive shifts over the long term. Rome was not built in a day – neither were you! So forget what others think of you, forget what you have previously expected of yourself and raise your bar. Compete with your own personal best and as you gradually improve your thinking, your goals will unfold before you. And remember no matter what is going on in your world you must expect the best, plan for the worst and prepared to be surprised.

How to incorporate this wisdom into your life

Like so much of what really matters in our life, the challenge with expectations is that they are, to a large extent, unconscious. There are some situations where you may sit around worrying about the outcome and certainly that's not going to help bring about a positive outcome. But it's even harder to bring about a positive outcome when your expectations are so low that you aren't even aware of them.

The first thing you have to do is role-play the situations you face. Imagine the best possible outcome over and over again. Say, for example, you are giving an important presentation at work. Role-play the presentation. Rehearse it with other people present and on your own. Imagine all the possible questions you could be asked so that you are prepared for them if and when they arise. Going over what could happen and imagining the best possible outcome will have a positive effect on your results and will give you confidence to deliver the best possible performance.

Chapter 20

When one's expectations are reduced to zero, one really appreciates everything one does have. ~ Stephen Hawking

Stephen Hawking is a British theoretical physicist who has worked on the basic laws that govern the universe. Along with Roger Penrose he has shown that Einstein's General Theory of Relativity implied space and time would have a beginning in the Big Bang and an end in black holes. This means that Einstein was correct in thinking that there must be a unified theory that would unite General Relativity with Quantum Theory, the other great scientific development of the first half of the 20th century. At 21 Hawking was diagnosed with Motor Neurone Disease, a progressive degenerative disease that leads to weakness and wasting of muscles.

Following on the heels of the previous chapter, this quote may seem contradictory at first glance. After all, I was quoting Denis Waitley saying that our outcomes are largely dependant on our expectations of those outcomes. If we expect to fail we increase our chances of failure exponentially! Conversely, if we expect to win we increase our chances of winning to the same degree.

Stephen Hawking is also talking about expectations only his focus is on gratitude. Stephen Hawking is without question one of the most brilliant thinkers of our time and yet he was born into a body which has progressively degenerated to the point he can no longer talk without a voice synthesiser and he has been confined to a wheelchair for most of his adult life.

Speaking about his disability he said, *The realisation that I had an incurable disease, that was likely to kill me in a few years, was a bit of a shock. How could something like that happen to me? Why should I be cut off like this? However, while I had been in hospital, I had seen a boy I vaguely knew die of leukaemia, in the bed opposite me. It had not been a pretty sight. Clearly there were people who were worse off than me. At least my condition didn't make me feel sick. Whenever I feel inclined to be sorry for myself I remember that boy'.*

And this is exactly what Hawking is talking about when he refers to having no expectations. His body has degenerated so much that his expectations about what he can do for himself have been reduced to zero and yet he is still managing to make a massive contribution to the world. Thus far, he has lived a full and purposeful life; he has three children and is still active in his search for a unifying theory.

Things don't always seem fair and I can't imagine how frustrating it must be to have a mind as active and brilliant as his and not be able to speak! But life isn't meant to be fair and no one ever said it was! His very real physical disability has not stopped Hawking living a full life.

In my own life, it is very easy for me to slip into feelings of isolation, loneliness, sadness and despair. In particular, there are certain times of the year that I still feel the devastation of losing my mum as if it were yesterday. Traditional family times such as Christmas, Mother's Day, Easter and birthdays are particularly hard. But some truly wonderful people surround me and I am comforted and strengthened by the amazing things in my life too. I live in one of the most incredible countries in the world. I am grateful for the opportunity to create a business I am passionate about and grateful for the friendships I have and the laughter those people bring into my world.

And as I sit back and write this chapter during the holiday season, I am particularly reminded of a woman that I met in 2007, Violet Li, whose journey has been a real inspiration to me. Death is an inevitable part of life – we will all die at some point; it is the great equaliser of man. However, the inevitability never seems to make the letting go any easier or the pain any less acute. The more we love, the more it hurts. The only comfort we can take is the knowledge that the pain is worth it in some small way – for if we had not loved so deeply in the first place, our hearts would not ache when loved ones pass away.

I have had a few losses over the course of my lifetime and I can assure you that more practice doesn't make it any easier. Sometimes I actually feel like I am getting worse at saying goodbye and letting go, not better. Violet Li, however, is a truly amazing woman and has been an inspiration to me in this regard. She has been through so much and endured so many losses, yet she has a vibrancy and courage that would put most people to shame. At the age of only ten, she lost her mother. In 1999, at the age of 29, she was left paraplegic after a motor vehicle accident that also claimed the life of her fiancé. And only shortly thereafter in 2000, she also lost her brother and father to a brain tumour and cancer, respectively.

Despite the unbelievable odds, the bereavement and the physical restrictions, Violet is not a woman without hope or purpose. She is one of the most generous, talented, beautiful and amazing women I've ever met. She has moved on with her life – met and married her adoring husband Boris and is a successful image consultant on the Gold Coast. And the one thing that stands out to me is her ability to appreciate and be truly grateful for the things that she does have, instead of focusing on what she does not have.

Did you know ... ?

Einstein said, 'thank you' at least 100 times every single day. He used to like to thank all of the scientists that came before him – their contributions allowed him to achieve so much more in his own life.

Wayne Dyer also talks of the importance of gratitude in *Manifest Your Destiny*. Gratitude is an attitude of thankfulness even when things don't work out as you'd hoped. We can never know all the cause-and-effect relationships that weave their way through our life and how we weave our way through other people's lives. As a result gratitude is about being grateful for what we do have, suspending judgement and recognising that while we may not always get everything we want, we always get everything we need in order for us to grow and develop.

It is impossible to bring more of what you want into your life if you are feeling ungrateful about what you already have. It has been said that the whole is more than the sum of its parts. In many ways gratitude is a bit like that – it's not what you say, the mere words that count, but sum of the words and the heartfelt emotion behind them.

Think about it. When we lose someone we love, suffer disappointment or feel hurt by others, we tend to get very angry, complain to anyone who will listen or vow revenge. However, like a coin, every emotion has an equal and opposite side – a flip side if you will. Have you ever stopped to think about the flip side of a negative emotion that you or someone else has experienced? Those negative emotions and their flip sides serve a very important purpose in that they provide the catalyst and mechanism for us to grow as individuals, become more flexible, gain tolerance, develop courage, exercise creativity and increase our understanding of ourselves and the world around us.

Even so, we never seem to greet challenges and obstacles with a sense of enthusiasm, excitement and anticipation. If we did, our friends would surely commit us! But the flip side of many of these important hardships and life lessons is often for our greater good and highest purpose. The British author GK Chesterton once said *'Do not free the camel of the burden of its hump, you may be freeing him from being a camel'.*

I can only speak for myself. Looking back on my own life, there have been so many times when I pleaded with God to save me from my burdens and struggles. If things could be undone and I had been rescued, would I be the same person that I am today? It is difficult to say with any great degree of certainty whether the new me, without the hump, would be any better or worse. But I can say with conviction, that I wouldn't be ME. As much as I wish things could have been different, I accept that it is the painful experiences of my life that have shaped and sculpted me far more eloquently than any quick fix or divine intervention ever could. In an ironic way, I would owe my deepest gratitude to every difficult challenge that I have ever faced, for it is those tests that have moulded my character.

Without a doubt, one of the most powerful lessons that I have learned in my journey is the power of gratitude. Gratitude is not something that you do once in awhile, it needs to be part of the fabric of your everyday life – something you do consistently with heartfelt meaning. That means reminding yourself of all the good things in your life. The simple process of searching for and finding the positive despite any negative that may exist will ensure you don't take the gifts and blessings in your life for granted. And that will bring you even more of what you do want.

How to incorporate this wisdom into your life

Make gratitude a 'richual' — something that you do consistently that enriches your life. Find something in your daily routine that you do time and again — picking up your car keys, petting your cat or dog, tying your shoelaces, turning the light on or off, printing a document at work, going into your kitchen. Ideally this activity needs to be something that you do often but doesn't require you to concentrate so your mind is free to create your 'richual'. Once you have selected something, make it a 'richual' to verbalise three things that you are grateful for each time you touch that object or perform that routine task. Choose different things throughout the day that you are grateful for.

This simple shift in your energy will have two effects: (1) it will change your outlook on the day by putting you in a more positive state of mind and (2) your subconscious mind will begin to focus on and filter for what you are grateful for and want more of in your life, as opposed to all your complaints and problems.

The process of being grateful for everything that you already have can also be extrapolated and used in your goal setting. Back in Chapter 10, you set some new goals for yourself. And as part of that process, we ended each goal by stating 'I give thanks to the abundance of the universe for my incredible gifts, health, abundance and good fortune'. When you appreciate and give thanks as though you have already received the goal, you are giving a strong signal to your subconscious mind that you have already achieved the goal. The goal is not to be achieved somewhere in the future, it is achieved in the here and now. And since the subconscious mind can only act on what it believes to be true (regardless of whether it actually is yet or not), you will have engaged the most powerful part of your brain in attracting the people, resources, events and opportunities necessary to bring that goal to fruition quickly and easily.

Chapter 21

Take away the cause, and the effect ceases. ~ Miguel De Cervantes

> Miguel De Cervantes was a Spanish novelist, poet and playwright. Considered one of the most influential people in literature he was the leading figure associated with the cultural flourishing of 16th century Spain. His novel Don Quixote in widely believed to be a founding classic of Western literature and regularly figures among the best novels ever written. It has been translated into more than 65 languages.

In life we either have results or we have reasons. There is no in-between. If you don't like the results you have produced, you will do one of two things (1) find a reason or excuse to explain why or (2) change your behaviour to produce a different result. Stated differently, you are either at the effect of, or at cause for everything that happens in your world.

To the extent you are pointing to reasons (persons or circumstances over which you have no control) then you have given up all your power and you have no hope of changing your circumstance. We often find ourselves saying things like – I can't lose weight because my spouse or kids eat too much junk food, I can't be successful because I am too old to try something new, my business failed because my employees didn't work hard enough, I failed the test because the room was too warm and I got too nervous, I can't start my own business because the economy is bad, I can't stop smoking because my spouse smokes two packs a day etc. Does any of this sound familiar to you? Looking for justification as to why things have not worked out is a pointless exercise – it will never assist you to achieve the results you desire because it is focused on the reason rather than on finding a solution to the challenge at hand.

When we look at causes, rather than reasons, things are very different. There is no failure, only results. Essentially, it means never having a reason or excuse again. Sounds scary, doesn't it? At first blush, this is a hard pill to swallow for most people.

Looking at causes is not about blaming or kicking yourself for attracting a mess into your life – it's about taking control of and systematically eliminating reasons and excuses that stand in the way of getting the results that you desire. And remember, reasons can come in the guise of negative emotions or states of mind, limiting beliefs, blame, any external justification, conflicting values, or attitudes that simply do not serve you.

On some level, I believe that we choose or create everything that is in our world. Like all beliefs, this theory can neither be proven nor disproved – it is simply something that I choose to live my life by. It isn't really important whether you agree or not the point I'm making is that what you believe only matters in so far as it directly influences your results. So if you are not getting the outcome you want, why not change what you believe and see if that alters your results! Your beliefs produce either good or bad results, they both support you and add confidence to you or they detract from your ability to interact with the world. If what you currently believe does not empower you to consistently produce what you want most in life, then isn't now the best time to change?

Under my belief system, I create and attract everything in my world. So even if I have results that I do not like, the good news is that I can 'un-create' or 'un-choose' to have it again in the future through my actions or non-actions. The process of un-choosing or re-choosing is very simple – by systematically removing the reasons and excuses, I can step up and recreate the world in the likeness of my dreams and imagination.

The years after my mom's death were a very dark time for me – I blamed others for my depression and poor health, I was angry, I felt cheated, I stopped moving forward with my life, I spent my time looking for reasons why this had happened to me and I kept my distance from others because I felt ashamed of what had happened in my family.

Did you know ... ?

We have all heard of the idea of Karma – we reap what we sow, we get what we give. Everything we do in our life has consequences that we will have to pay for at some point in our evolution. No debt goes unpaid in the universe and therefore it's imperative that we can learn to step back from our choices and assess them in this light. If we behave badly to someone we will pay a comparative price for that behaviour. By learning not to rely on conditioned responses and instead take conscious control of the decisions and actions we take we are able to ensure that we learn the lessons we are meant to learn so we can move on instead of continuously repeating them.

In his astonishing book *The Adventure of Self-Discovery* Dr Stanislav Grof, former Chief of Psychiatric Research at the Maryland Psychiatric Research Center, talks about the presence of a link between forgiveness and karma. He identified that individuals would often highlight a protagonist in their lives and direct blame and unresolved anger toward that person. What was amazing, however, was once the individual had found resolution, and had taken responsibility for their part in the situation and forgiven the other person, something miraculous happened to both parties. It seemed that in a very tangible way the idea of the little soul in the sun is real and not just metaphorical! Two souls had made a pact to teach each other something and once even one of them was able to take responsibility for that (even if they didn't fully understand the karmic pattern) they were able to get the lesson and move on spiritually and emotionally.

Grof set about to verify these findings and was able to show that when one person made a significant breakthrough in terms of forgiveness and taking responsibility for their part in the situation, a dramatic shift occurred not just in that person but also in the 'protagonist' – even if they were separated by thousands of miles! The timing of these transformational events was often just minutes apart, pointing to some form of nonlocal communication where there was a mutual understanding that some karmic debt had just been cancelled. Both 'victim' and 'protagonist' were miraculously able to move on in their lives.

I have been so fortunate to discover that there is a reason for all things – even those that are senseless and incomprehensible – and that we have to somehow learn to trust that there is a bigger picture that perhaps we, as mere human beings, can never truly understand. The most beautiful expression of this idea I've ever read was in a children's book *Little Soul in the Sun* by Neil Donald Walsh (author of *Conversations with God*). In the story, Walsh talks of a Little Soul who wants to be incarnated as a human being to learn 'forgiveness'. A Friendly Soul agrees to oblige him by incarnating as a person to do something to the Little Soul that will help him learn the lesson of forgiveness. But the Friendly Soul issues a plea of caution and says, *'at the very moment that I strike you down, please promise me that you will remember who I really am, a Friendly and loving Soul, otherwise we will be doomed to repeat the process over and over again until we get the learnings or until another Little Soul comes down to help us find the way out'.*

In other words everything that happens in our life – the good the bad and the just plain ugly is the result of an agreement that we have made at some point in our existence to experience certain things so we can become better human beings and move on to the next lesson. On some level, we are all doing the best that we can with the resources that we think we have available. Everything is a learning experience and if viewed from that context, we can be empowered to create a world around us in the likeness of our dreams and wildest imaginations. Even the really hard stuff happens for a reason. There is no failure, only results. It isn't about assigning blame or beating yourself up – it's about being responsible for your response and deciding how best to move forward to attract the results that you want.

Blaming others – even if it's legitimate – robs you of your power. It doesn't help you move on – it's a complete waste of your time and emotion. Put it in the past and find a way to ensure you never repeat it. Forget finding a fall guy – you and only you are responsible for your life so step up to the plate and swing the bat. As Wayne Gretzky once said, *'You miss 100% of the shots you never take'.*

Life doesn't change – we change. The only way to be the change that you want to see in the world is to take responsibility for the life that you say you want to be living. Regardless of the events and circumstances that have occurred, no answers may be found revelling in excuses.

Looking back, forgiveness has been a major theme in my life. I've struggled with it in many contexts throughout my childhood, adolescence and adult life. There are so many hurts and grievances I have held onto for decades and a few I still struggle with letting go of. And I know that they bind me to the past like an umbilical cord binds an unborn child to his mother.

I find it difficult to forgive. Perhaps I am not alone? I can't decide some days who is more difficult to forgive – others or myself? I am no doubt a slow learner and my life has patiently provided lesson after lesson that I might truly know myself as 'forgiveness'.

I may never forget what has happened but I do believe that we can all move beyond our past and create a life of purpose and significance by being the cause for everything in our lives, rather than just living with life's effects. And the only question you really need to ask yourself is 'does what you currently believe allow you to live the life you were truly meant to live?' If it doesn't, make the change today. You've already waited long enough!

How to incorporate this wisdom into your life

If you are currently living with effects in any aspect of your life, you must seek out the cause. If that effect is not something you want, then finding the underlying cause will give you the power to change your world. As De Cervantes correctly surmised, *'If you remove the cause the effect will cease'*.

Learn to be a master of spin. One of the most useful things to come out of politics in the last few years is the art of spin. Spin is essentially re-packaging of the truth to find a benefit in a negative story!

If it works in politics why not apply it you your own life? The next time you find yourself at the effect of something negative, imagine you're the head of the country and you need to deliver a press release about what's just happened and you must find a way to turn it around and appear completely in charge of the situation. Once you've found a spin that works – even if it just makes you laugh or it seems outlandish or implausible – apply it to your situation and move forward. Get on the cause side of the equation and make the necessary changes now so you can attract the results you want or extract something positive from the situation.

Chapter 22

Come to the edge', we say. 'We are afraid', they say. 'Come to the edge,' we say. And they come. And they look. And we push. And they fly. We to stay and die in our beds. They to go and die howsoever, yet inspiring those who come after them to find their own edge. And fly. ~ Guillaume Apollinaire

Guillaume Apollinaire was a French poet and writer. Among the foremost poets of the early 20th century, he is credited with coining the word surrealism. Apollinaire wrote an optimistic manifesto called 'The New Spirit and the Poets' which following his death remains his parting word. In it he spoke of his universal belief in scientific exploration and the need to look at the very big as well as the very small. He claimed that, 'The altered conception of the world will necessarily bring on fresh ideas and new means of expression, breaking with antiquated tradition.' And that artists should make use of a reality that sometimes exceeds legend!

Sometimes in life we are either coaxed to the edge and pushed off or we willingly wander there oblivious to what lies ahead. Either is good – at the moment your feet leave the safety of the cliff top – you will always find your wings.

My first experience of this was as a result of a part-time job I had selling shoes at the local mall when I was 14. That role led me to another part-time job at the Hudson Bay Company (HBC) where I was part of the Bay Teen Council. This organisation was formed to give a select group of girls the opportunity to learn modelling skills, participate in community-based activities and work in various positions at the HBC.

I was fortunate enough to be promoted into the customer service cash office where I was given the opportunity to learn new skills and undertake significant financial responsibility. The General Manager of the store, Rod Turnbull, took a real shine to me. He was the President of the local Rotary Club and it was through him that I was given the opportunity in 1984 to attend high school for one year in Hokkaido, Japan.

At the time I didn't know a single word in Japanese but I was absolutely, positively committed to going on the exchange. I had no idea of the magnitude of what I had undertaken until I landed on the northern island of Japan, completely exhausted from over 24 hours of travelling on my own. The city that had been chosen for me was almost identical in size to my hometown and very similar in terms of climate. Alberta and Hokkaido are actually sister provinces. What I didn't know at the time was that I was the sole foreign resident. There were a few missionaries and visitors but they didn't reside in Eniwa City full time.

At 5"8' with blonde hair and blue, eyes I stood out in the crowd! I couldn't go anywhere without causing a stir – people would follow me, touch my hair or just stare. Even an appointment to get my hair cut made the local papers as a newsworthy event. Some of the residents had never actually seen a foreigner in real life. However, my conspicuous physical appearance was the least of my worries – I didn't speak a word of Japanese and for the most part, my hosts did not speak English either! At least not fluently. My immersion started immediately – I arrived at the school on my first day and was mobbed by the other students. They were extremely gentle but they all wanted to get up close to touch my hair and impress me with their command of English by saying 'This is a pen'. Nothing else, just 'this is a pen', over and over. It was quite adorable and endearing. I recognised quickly that I was going to have to learn the language in order to get by.

It was incredibly hot and humid – it rained non-stop the first week that I was there. I remember that week so clearly, especially the day that I realised I was in way over my head. I had been nudged out of the nest and as I began to feel the sensation of falling my heart began to race and I quickly realised that the time had come for me to spread my wings. It happened in an instant … they unfolded and it was the most natural and effortless feeling. I felt incredibly supported and safe even though it was the first time that I had been outside of North America. I was alone in a country where everyone looked different, spoke a language I couldn't understand and ate raw fish for dinner and yet somehow, I felt strangely at home.

Looking back, I am so glad that I didn't know what it would be like before I got on that plane. I am quite sure if I did, I never would have gone and I would have missed out on one of my most valuable experiences.

There was no doubt that I was in way over my head but somehow that height was exactly what I needed to measure my spirit and soar with the eagles on the adventure of a lifetime. I was fully committed and there was no turning back. Rod Turnbull had lured me to the edge – he pushed and I flew.

And in a heartbeat, a world like I have never seen or known before unfolded beneath me, steeped in all its history, mystique and magnificence. I opened my mind and my heart to a people and a culture that was diametrically opposed to anything that I had ever encountered before. My hosts – families, friends, teachers, Rotary club members, the community at large – embraced me with a sense of love, understanding, curiosity, encouragement, support and generosity that I have never experienced before or since. I have the utmost gratitude, respect and love for every single person that touched my life during those memorable 12 months. I had a once in a lifetime opportunity to see the country, experience the traditions (tea ceremony, flower arrangement, Koto, traditional dance, cooking), learn the language and gain a real insight into the true essence of the people.

Without question, this experience at 17 left an indelible impression on my heart and soul. The experience of taking the leap of faith and finding the wind beneath my wings has enabled me to remain strong and steadfast despite the many storms and tempests that I faced in later life.

Sometimes it's best not to know what's around the corner … if we did, we may never take the next step. But Apollinaire was right – we do fly. Even when we are sure that we will hit the ground at 200 km/h, somehow we find something inside that we never knew was there and everything is different from that moment onward.

Did you know ... ?

According to body weight and the laws of aerodynamics it should be impossible for the bumblebee to fly. Luckily for the bumblebee, no one told him and so he continues to travel three metres per second, beating his little wings 130 times. He's completely oblivious to the laws of anything other than pollination. This story has become firmly rooted in self-help folklore but is it really true.

It is possible that the story first surfaced in Germany in the 1930s. One evening at dinner, a prominent aerodynamicist happened to be talking to a biologist, who asked about the flight of bees. To answer the biologist's query, the engineer did a quick 'back-of-the-napkin' calculation. Assuming for simplicity sake a rigid, smooth wing, he estimated the bee's weight and wing area, and calculated the lift generated by the wing. Not surprisingly, there was insufficient lift. You just have to look at the bee's rotund body in relation to his wings to know that theoretically he might have problems.

Whether this or any of the other theories of origin are true or not isn't really relevant. What is relevant is that the bumblebee can fly and perhaps more importantly that there will always be a difference between a 'thing' and a mathematical model of a 'thing'. As living creatures and legends go, the bumblebee is as much a mystery as ever and we can all fly if we just stretch our wings.

At the time in 1984, I had never heard of Apollinaire or his famous words and I suppose it didn't really matter because I had learned to fly as so many of us do. Ironically, a time would come many years later, in 1993, when I desperately needed to hear those words and be coaxed back to my own edge so that I might fly once again.

In July 1993, Gary Kovacs introduced me to Apollinaire's words in a book that holds a special place in my heart – *All I Needed to Know I Learned in Kindergarten* by Robert Fulgrum. It was a very important day for me – the day that I was admitted to the Law Society of Alberta – but it was also one of mixed emotions. Just over a year had passed since I lost my mother. It was a year of firsts but not the kind that you want to remember. I had to endure my first mother's day, first Christmas, first birthday, first Thanksgiving, university graduation and now this, all without her.

I wanted to feel happy and proud and keep up appearances for all of my guests on the day. Many had come long distances to support me on that day and wanted to show their love and encouragement. I was so grateful for that, but to be honest, I was struggling just to make it through the day. I didn't want to be there and I certainly didn't feel like celebrating – I was just going through the motions. For me this ceremony, like my life, had in many ways just become a formality. Something I did because I had to. But I had lost the will to fly … I was too scared to leave the nest now for fear of falling or of losing someone else that I loved. I curled up inside of the safety of what I knew – where I was alone but where I had the illusion of certainty and protection.

I had a number of guests over to my home afterwards for drinks and canapés. I expected everyone to leave after only a few hours but the celebration took on a life of its own. Gary, as usual, had become the life of the party and had cranked up the stereo to its maximum capacity. He had turned my living room into a dance floor – he was jumping around like an absolute idiot, singing away to 54-40 at the top of his lungs. Under any other circumstances, I probably would have joined in – threw caution to the wind and really let my hair down. But it had been a long time since I felt like smiling, let alone dancing and celebrating.

I tried everything to get him to stop – I was so incredibly pissed off and indignant with his behaviour. I just wanted him to stop and go home – I couldn't believe how insensitive he was to how I was feeling. But he knew exactly what I was feeling – he always did. He had an uncanny way of seeing right through me and managing to put his finger on exactly what was going on. He knew me very well back then– maybe better than I knew myself. He was incredibly perceptive and he didn't pull any punches. I trusted him implicitly.

He took me outside, away from all the others so that we could have a private conversation. He pulled out a special card that he had written for me on this occasion – a card that contained some private words of encouragement and support plus the famous quote from Apollinaire:

'And they come. And they look. And we push. And they fly. We to stay and die in our beds. They to go and die howsoever, yet inspiring those who come after them to find their own edge. And fly'.

And he said, *'As I sat there in the courthouse today I couldn't help but feel proud for all that you have accomplished. As I listened to Justice Rooke re-count your journey – especially the last 14 months which have been so heart wrenching – I looked around the room and was left with the overwhelming impression that you have touched and been an inspiration to so many with your courage and tenacity. The girl that I knew before this happened didn't sit out the dance on the sidelines, with the stereo turned down to a 'reasonable' level, watching the world pass her by. She wasn't afraid of getting hurt, taking risks and soaring with the eagles. And the time will come, one day very soon, when you will find yourself back at the edge. And I will push. And you will fly'.*

And he was right. There comes a point in everyone's life when it is time to stop grieving or worrying and commence living again. If there is anything that life has taught me it is that, regardless of what has happened in the past or where you are now, 'it's never too late to fly'.

How to incorporate this wisdom into your life

Do something you've never done before at least once a year. Take up tap dancing classes, join a charity expedition and climb Kilimanjaro, join Toastmasters or cycle through Asia. Instead of lying on a beach this year on holiday volunteer to look after elephants in Africa. Doing something that stretches you physically, emotionally and/or spiritually – it is a great way to test out your wings!

Find a way to stretch beyond what you would ever do yourself. You will be surprised of what you're really capable of when you face your fear and do it anyway!

Chapter 23

Courage is not the absence of fear, but rather the judgment that something else is more important than fear. ~ Ambrose Redmoon

Ambrose Redmoon was a pseudonym for James Neil Hollingworth – Born in Painesville, Ohio, he was a beatnik, hippie, writer and manager of the psychedelic folk rock band Quicksilver Messenger Service. Known for his outrageous, wild and confronting style, he was never published and was not known during his lifetime beyond a small circle of mystics and followers of neo-paganism. After a tragic car accident that left him paralysed and in a wheelchair, he spent the last years of his life in a garage apartment in Santa Rosa, California.

Isn't it interesting how both the words 'courage' and 'fear' tend to consistently show up in sentences where the definition of courage is postulated? It is as if the two are inextricably linked – that fear (or fearlessness) is somehow a necessary pre-cursor to courage.

What exactly is courage and how does one obtain it? Personally I think it's a complicated, misunderstood and elusive human virtue. We tend to want to define it in terms of deeds or circumstances — we think of it as something that we do once in a while rather than who we are as human beings. It is more common for courage to be defined by example than by abstract explanation. For example, if you ask anyone on the street to define courage, they would be more likely to respond with 'courage is going into a burning building to save a child' rather than 'courage is an admirable personality trait characterised by the ability to act regardless of the potential consequences'.

The debate about whether courage is linked to fear has a long history dating back to the days of Plato and Aristotle. Aristotle thought that actually feeling fear was integral to courage, whereas Plato argued that it was the rational understanding of fear, rather than allowing oneself to actually feel the feeling, that was critical. I'm with Plato.

I have no doubt that fear often exists at the very moment when we are called upon to have courage but I believe that real courage is not a gut reaction but a conscious choice. Take, for example, Benazir Bhutto. She was assassinated on 27 December 2007 after returning to Pakistan. She was granted amnesty after having corruption charges withdrawn by President Pervez Musharraf. She displayed incredible courage, knowing full well that her return would put her life in danger and she sacrificed her life for her beloved country. She could easily have remained in the comfort or safety of London or Dubai but she chose to return to her country to run for office in the hope that she could make a difference.

We live in a world where atrocities such as terrorism, genocide, war, child pornography, poverty and female circumcision etc., are reported every day in the news. We are justifiably terrified, disgusted and outraged but we are also often numbed into a state of helplessness and complacency – we like to think that these are things that happen to other people on the other side of the world. It seems that it is only when these external fears come closer to home, do we find the courage necessary to step in. But those such as Benazir Bhutto stepped in anyway and that takes real courage.

If you look back on your life, I am sure you will agree that there may have been hundreds of times when you experienced the emotion of fear but did not summon the courage to take action and do something about it. Fears are a dime a dozen: courage, however, is a far more precious and elusive commodity. Conversely, there may even be times where you acted courageously and were not even aware, until afterwards, that you felt or should have felt fear. You acted on instinct and simply did what was necessary in the moment. There is no causative link between fear or fearlessness and courage.

When I lost my mother back in 1992, I struggled to find the courage to do what I needed to do and move on with my life. But fear wasn't a huge motivating factor. At the time, I felt that I had already lost almost everything that mattered or underpinned who I was – my sense of home and family. There was nothing left to be afraid of, I had already hit rock bottom. I remember feeling overwhelmed with grief, loneliness, anger, shock and despair; it was like walking around in a cloud of darkness that felt like it would never lift. At the time, I simply could not imagine that in time the hurt would fade, my heart would heal and I would once again re-engage with life. In that moment, courage chose me, not the other way around – I had no other choice.

Many people have told me that they think that I am incredibly courageous to have survived that period in my life. I never thought of it that way because I felt I didn't have a choice in the matter. I did what I did in order to survive – I didn't have the time or the energy to sit around contemplating my fears or weighing up the potential consequences. My natural instincts took over and I simply did what was necessary in the circumstances. Looking back, fear or fearlessness never factored. I just remember knowing that I felt that I had to give my mother the tribute she deserved at her funeral, I had to see that justice was served, I had to complete my articles for law so that she would be proud, I had to find a way to re-establish a home and build a new family. For me, these things represented a greater calling. I don't think of it as courage but rather necessity.

Strangely enough, I regard the decision to move to Australia, or the one I made to write this book, far more courageous. With these, I had a choice. I had the luxury of time to reflect on the options, weigh up the consequences, examine my feelings and identify a greater mission.

I worked long and hard to put my past behind me. I locked up a piece of my life, put it in a box and moved 20,000 kilometres away for a new start in Australia. The process of writing this book has brought so many of the emotions and memories back to the surface, I am recalling thoughts and feelings that I haven't contemplated in years. I am also very cognisant of the effect that my writing about these events may have on others in my life – that they may see it as a re-surfacing of issues and hurts that are better left covered up and buried.

Truth be told, I have been thinking about writing this book for over 14 years. There are so many things that I want to say and share – lessons that

I have learned, distinctions that have made the world of difference and a message of hope for others who have suffered terrible loss or simply lost their way. But yet, I was immobilised by fear and that fear prevented me from starting this project for many years. The fear of dredging up the past and also the fear that what I would have to say would drive me even further apart from what little family I still have.

Even as I write this, I am extremely torn and as the book enters its final stages the feeling has intensified. On one hand, I feel a strong pull toward this new direction in my life. I genuinely feel that my experiences are not to be buried away. I have come to appreciate that 'letting sleeping dogs lie' is never a useful long-term resolution. But more than that, I want people to see from my experiences and those of other people I mention that it doesn't matter what happens to us we always have the opportunity to choose the meaning that we will ascribe to it.

On the other hand, I am torn by an immense sense of obligation to carry the secrets in silence. The last thing I want to do is harm my remaining family – my brother or my father. Despite everything that has happened, they are my flesh and blood and I love them despite all the pain and heartache. Although I don't have regular contact with either of them and don't have the kind of relationship I'd like to have, I think they have both taken strides to rebuild their lives and move on. And I am fearful that the disconnection I already feel from them will become absolute after this book is written.

My whole life I was brought up under the mantra that 'what happens at home is private and not talked about outside to anyone'. As kids we were punished for speaking up. There were times when I confided in my grandparents about the alcoholism and abuse that we suffered at home. I learned very quickly that the repercussions for breaking the code of silence were severe. We grew up under an insidious cloud of secrecy – even now I feel the pressure to keep this information to myself in order to 'protect' the family.

Sadly I don't think my family was really that different from millions of others around the world. One of the reasons that domestic violence, alcohol and drug additions, neglect and sexual crimes are so prevalent is that the victims are often afraid to leave or speak out for fear of the ramifications.

I did not write this book as revenge or to attack either my brother or my father. There are actually events I have deliberately left out because there was little to be gained by their inclusion. I don't blame either of them because what is done is done but sooner or later we all have to take responsibility for our actions and our lives. And that includes me. In the end I have to choose the path I feel most compelled toward. I had to have the courage in my conviction that this book could help many more people than its creation would hurt. I had to have the courage to do what I felt was right and know in my heart that my continued silence was helping no one.

Did you know ... ?

The word courage comes from the French word, *coeur*, which means heart. This etymology is particularly insightful in that the heart is usually associated with the emotion of love. This parallels the meaning in the Hebrew language – '*ometz lev*', or literally, '*strength of heart*'.

The heart is not an organ that pumps blood, then rests and later resumes beating. It is characterised by its continuous and unremitting rhythm. With the heart as the sustaining organ, it follows that all courage is grounded in the steadfast and unrelenting life force of love. Courage is not bred of fear or fearlessness but rather by the unyielding embrace of a calling that is far greater than fear.

We will all experience fear in our life. It is as necessary for our evolution as breathing. For me I had to survive and courage will emerge in times of survival – be that from losing someone you love or being diagnosed with a serious illness. Courage is what makes us fight instead of give up. We have to learn to accept fear as part of our life. Often it sits permanently below the surface: The fear of failing in a new job or business, the fear of saying 'no' to others, the fear of expressing our true feelings, the fear of letting our family down, the fear of standing up for what we believe in or the fear of standing by someone who is being ridiculed or chastised for their appearance, race or religion. While these may not be life or death situations they are no less daunting or debilitating. Regardless of what is causing the fear in these 'moments of truth' it is the mysterious capacity for courage that allows us to dig deep and find the ability to pursue what is right and just, despite the fact that the journey may be long and the path unclear.

Fear is a natural part of being human and necessary for our survival. It is, however, only meant to temper our choices so we consciously engage with our environment. It isn't meant to grind us to a halt. As we grow up fear is channelled into other areas and can result in a manipulation of an elemental force. We learn to suppress it, ignore it, cover it up, magnify it, leverage it and some of us even learn how to harness it. These behaviours are all directed at either anesthetising fear, or becoming fearless, but they do not create courage or propel us towards courage, rather they are a distraction.

Looking to our fears for answers about to how to gain courage is a bit like getting in our car and attempting to drive down the freeway by only looking into the rear view mirror. Fear is always in the opposite direction of where you want to go. Or as Jack Canfield, best selling co-author of the *Chicken Soup for the Soul* series puts it, *'Everything you want is on the other side of fear'.* The answer to the question – how do we find courage – lies in finding a calling that is much greater than fear. Doing what needs to be done despite the fear and finding a meaning that makes it make some sense.

In many ways, courage is a choice. It is like a door that is always available to be opened. It is not a commodity that we store up or build over time for future use – although exercising it does make it easier in times of crisis. Having had courage in the past does not guarantee it in the future; the converse is also true.

Most of us assume that because we may not have exercised courage in the past, it means that we are not courageous or capable of courage. This is a fallacy. You have the ability to choose courage every single day. The key is not in the belief that you have what it takes to overcome the fear but rather that you see in the distance something so amazing, essential or desirable that you are simply compelled to take a step toward it. To embrace courage is to embrace a calling far greater than fear.

How to incorporate this wisdom into your life

It takes courage of heart to go deeper into the questions of who you are and who you want to be in the world. One of the most powerful things that people can do is read good books. When you read stories of courage you begin to wonder how you might have coped in the same circumstances. We are often humbled by the strength and courage of the hero of the story who has often faced obstacles far greater than our own and it inspires us to choose courage and move beyond our limitations towards something far greater. These stories have a way of capturing our hearts, overtaking our emotions and arousing great courage – they are essentially 'cries of the heart'.

If you are dedicated to achieving a certain goal then the best use of your time would be to seek out biographies of people who have already achieved what you want. Find people who have done what you are trying to do and speak to them. By expanding your mind and understanding that courage is not a mystical quality available to a chosen few but a natural part of every one of us, then you can move confidently today toward your goals.

Chapter 24

All that we are is the result of what we have thought. The mind is everything. What we think, we become. ~ Buddha

Buddha or 'the Enlightened One' refers to Gautama Buddha, the founder of Buddhism. He was born into a royal family in the 6th century BC. As a young adult he sought spiritual answers and a greater understanding of life. Seeking guidance through meditation he achieved enlightenment and travelled far and wide to spread the path to salvation. After his death his pupils continued to spread his teachings and Buddhism is still very much alive today.

There are thousands of references to this idea – that our thinking influences our outcome. Ancient spiritual texts from the beginning of recorded history, either directly or indirectly call attention to the importance of thought. Hindu pre-Christian philosophy states, *'As a man acts so does he become. As a man's desire is, so is his destiny'*. Fourth century Greek philosophers talked of the importance of thought in manifesting desire into 'reality'. The Bible is also full of references such as, *'If ye shall have faith, nothing shall be impossible unto you'*. Kabbalistic texts also make reference to the connection between thought and experience. There is no religious thinking anywhere on the planet that says that what we think is irrelevant.

For the first time in history we are able to prove through empirical scientific study just how relevant our thoughts are. We are able to show that our thoughts do influence the world around us in a measurable way. What these sacred writings illustrated was not metaphorical but truth.

The emotionalised dominating thoughts we have on a habitual basis somehow impact the quantum field and influence the outcome. But don't get too excited – every passing fancy that you may have about how you would like your life to be will not suddenly materialise. The only thought with any power is long-term habitual, emotionalised thought.

The bad news is that most people don't apply long-term habitual emotionalised thought to anything positive. That sort of thinking is the domain of worry and anxiety. It's the type of thought that keeps you up at night for all the wrong reasons. Few of us ever learn to apply that habitual long-term thinking to positive outcomes.

It is this idea that is at the heart of the self-help classic *Think and Grow Rich*. Napoleon Hill was charged by wealthy industrialist Andrew Carnegie to study success. Through his connections Carnegie gave him unprecedented access to the great thinkers and leaders of the day and Hill researched what it was that made them successful. The result was a book that was, without question, the start of a billion dollar industry. What Hill found was that everyone who achieved anything remarkable had the ability to manage their thinking and direct their emotionalised dominating thoughts toward the desire they held in mind. This process has come to be known as visualisation and is an essential part of changing your world.

Australian psychologist Alan Richardson took three groups of basketball players and tested their ability to take free shots. He had the first group go on court and practise taking free shots for 20 minutes. He had the second group do nothing and the third group was to visualise shooting perfect baskets for 20 minutes a day. Unsurprisingly, the group that did nothing showed no improvement. The first group showed a 24% improvement but what was truly remarkable was that the third group showed a 23% improvement. Just by imagining the improvement through visualisation they were able to improve almost exactly the same amount as those that actually got on the court and practised.

Whether we realise it or not, we are visualising things all the time – visualising either what we want or don't want. Like a spider continually spinning a web, we are persistently thinking or imagining what might happen. If we are relentlessly focused on the negative outcome and are riddled by fear that WILL impact our reality.

Did you know … ?

Soviet athletes who took part in the 1980 Winter Games in Lake Placid New York had been involved in research between imagery and physical performance. The athletes had been divided into four groups prior to the competition. The first group spent 100% of their training time training. The second group spent 75% training and 25% visualising their improved performance. The third group spent 50% on each and the fourth group spent 25% training and 75% visualising. At the winter games, the group that showed the best performance was group four, followed by 3, 2 and 1 in that order.

Those that focused their mind and directed its awesome power toward a desired outcome showed a greater improvement than those that simply directed their body and practised in the traditional way.

A few years ago, before I really started to understand just how powerful our thoughts are in creating our reality, I was working for a company that was not financially stable. The head of finance was not a particularly ethical man and his political game-playing made it difficult to deal with him professionally. The company had a lot of money tied up in stale inventory and there was significant pressure to get this issue under control. A lot of the problems were attributable to inexperienced management, poor communication and a lack of accountability.

In light of what I witnessed, I began to get concerned about the financial viability of the company. I was a contractor and my monthly invoices were not being paid on time, which worried me. Inventory shipments were coming in from overseas and being unduly delayed on the dock because funds were tight. The head of finance began making little underhanded comments about not being able to afford my salary and not wanting me to be there. There was little I could do because I could not prove most of what he said. However, it really started to play on my mind and take its toll.

Before long I developed a very serious sinus infection. Due to the enormous work pressure, I was unable to take time off to rest – I was working about 65 hours a week. I became so ill that I was referred to two specialists – both of whom said it was one of the most severe cases they had ever seen. I was on antibiotics and anti-inflammatories for quite some time and had to have plastic surgery on the bridge of my nose. Despite this fact, I was receiving constant pressure to return to work immediately.

The niggling threats about my job and withholding pay weighed heavily on my mind. I found myself talking to my colleagues and friends about the issue constantly. I was consumed with fear and worry and I couldn't understand why this was happening to me. I would suppose that it is not very surprising that I was let go very shortly thereafter, without reason or proper notice. Whether I realised it or not at the time, I was constantly spinning the web of retrenchment that year in my own mind. I had seen several other very qualified, hard working and professional colleagues let go for no reason other than simple cost-cutting measures. It was a very real threat and possibility but I made it a reality by visualising it over and over again in my own mind. It didn't matter that it was not what I wanted to happen. What mattered was it became a habitualised emotional thought. What started off as a think became a thing – a thing that I really didn't want.

What we give energy to in our thoughts has a transformational magic that can bring those things about. The universal energy that makes this possible is still not fully understood but certainly the field of quantum physics is making great progress toward that end.

Regardless of whether the mechanics of this energy is understood the results are being proven time and again. And it seems that the force that transforms habitual emotional thought into reality will do so for positive or negative outcomes alike. So make sure you focus your thinking on what you want NOT on what you don't want.

I'll leave this point with the remarkable story of Mr Wright. Mr Wright had advanced cancer of the lymph nodes and was being treated by Bruno Klopfer. They had tried everything to no success and his time was clearly running out. Wright's neck, armpits, chest, abdomen and groin were filled with tumours the size of tennis balls. His spleen and liver were so enlarged that milky fluid had to be drained on a daily basis.

Wright had heard about a groundbreaking new drug called Krebiozen and was convinced it held the cure for his condition. He begged for the treatment and eventually his doctor accepted even though he felt sure it was too late. Wright on the other hand was adamant he had been given a lifeline. He made an astonishing recovery and Klopfer reported that his tumours had, 'melted like snowballs on a hot stove'. Ten days following his first treatment with the new drug Wright left hospital and was as far as the doctors could tell cancer free.

Wright remained well for two months and then articles began to appear about the validity of Krebiozen. This uncertainty affected Wright and he became depressed and suffered a relapse. He was re-admitted to hospital and in desperation the doctor reassured Wright about the potency of Krebiozen but that some of the initial supplies had deteriorated during shipping. He told Wright that a new highly concentrated version of the drug now existed and he could treat him with it immediately. Of course there was no new drug but Klopfer knew that whatever Wright was thinking was having a dramatic result on his body. The doctor went through an elaborate procedure and injected his patient with plain water.

Again the results were astonishing – even more so this time because there was no actual drug involved. The tumours dissolved and the chest fluid vanished and he was back on his feet again. Again he remained symptom free for two months but then the American Medical Association announced that a nationwide study of Krebiozen had found the drug worthless in the treatment of cancer. Wright was dead within two days.

Nothing had changed for Wright except one very important thing – his thinking! Be very careful what you focus your attention on – it could kill you.

How to incorporate this wisdom into your life

Stop worrying! We've always known that worrying doesn't help but now it is clear that worrying can actually make the possibility of whatever it is you worry about actually happen. By worrying about a particular eventuality with intensity and emotion you could actually be party to bringing it about. You need to break that pattern and focus your attention on the outcome you want to happen.

There is no quick fix for this, especially if you have been a habitual worrier. Just knowing that your obsessive stressing about what might go wrong is actually ensuring that it becomes more possible, is often enough to start people on the road to more positive thoughts. Consciously stop your worrying thoughts and instead immediately replace them with the most outrageous best-case scenario you can imagine. Have fun with it.

Chapter 25

*It is not whether your actions are tough or gentle; it is the spirit behind
your actions and words that announces your inner state.*
~ Chin-ning Chu

Chin-Ning Chu is a Chinese American business consultant involved
in helping Western business people interpret and translate some
of the business philosophies from the east. At 22 she left Taiwan
bound for the United States. All she had was a suitcase and two
little books, 'The Art of War' and 'Thick Black Theory' – sensing
both would be important to her in her new life. One of her most
successful books was Thick Face Black Heart. Throughout Asia and
Australia her books outsell the likes of Tom Peters and Anthony
Robbins!

I believe that the spirit behind your actions and words not only announces
your inner state but it influences the results you achieve in your life.
Various religious ideals can lead us to believe that we should do the right
thing because if we don't, when it's time for final judgement we will be
sent to hell.

What some proponents of religion are saying is that you should do the
right thing otherwise you will be punished. But if the only thing that
keeps you good is some possibility of eternal damnation then are you
really good or just scared? What is your predominant intention?

Intention is what really matters. Helping someone in crisis because you
think God might allocate you some brownie points is a very different
experience to helping someone in crisis because you recognise they need
help and want to make their life a little easier.

We have all had the misfortune of meeting insincere people. They say all the right words but something just doesn't add up. Their true intentions may never be overt but the mismatch between their words and actions is unmistakable.

Take racism for example. There are those that may never utter a racist comment in their entire lives and yet if you put them in a situation with people from different cultures their intention and opinion screams out at 1000 decibels. They may say lovely things yet their intention is not lovely at all. Conversely, you may hear two people speak in an appalling way to each other but there is no malice or racism implied. This is often the case in the African American community where they may choose to address each other using the 'N' word. To most people, that is an extremely offensive word. Yet used in this way it's not offensive to those involved because the unspoken intention behind the word is friendship and camaraderie. There is no malice.

Now I'm not saying for a second that anyone should ever use the word. I myself would not feel comfortable using under any circumstances. The point is, however, that it is the intention behind the actions and words that give them their true meaning and influence.

We need to appreciate the difference between our words and actions and the intention behind them. The intention will always win out. If you say you want something and you do the things that you think you need to do in order to manifest your goal and it still doesn't materialise, my guess is that your intention may not be congruent with your words and actions.

Unsurprisingly, the loss of my mother had a profound impact on my life. I became obsessed with the need to re-build a sense of stability and family. As is common to all those who experience the untimely loss of a much loved family member, once the initial grieving period has subsided, you are left with what feels like a massive hole in your heart. Speaking from experience, you will do anything to fill that emptiness … anything.

All of the usual poisons – eating, drinking, drugs, smoking, work, gambling, spending – are an inconsolable person's painkillers of choice. Many also resort to emotional self-deprivation (isolation, depression, anxiety, phobias), over-compensation, irrational behaviour (violence, revenge), or blame. No matter how much or how many of these you try, they are like air and none of them will ever fill the abyss.

I think Mae West once said, *'When faced with two evils, I always choose the one I haven't tried before'.* I can definitely relate to that statement. And not one to be outdone, I choose a few, to ensure I was sufficiently occupied. I suffered from severe depression and insomnia for about two years. I dropped from 130lbs down to 98lbs within weeks and I relied on sleeping pills and Prozac to get through my day. I was a complete mess, physically and emotionally. I couldn't bear the thought of putting food into my mouth, chewing and swallowing. The thought of it repulsed me. I was haunted by disturbing nightmares and spent a good many sleepless nights lying in bed and staring at the ceiling. During the day, I would often cry for hours uncontrollably but I made sure that I let everyone know that I was okay and doing much better. I bought myself a car, clothing, a house and I even travelled but nothing worked, I didn't feel any better. In the end I just withdrew from life.

After a year or two, I started to re-engage with people. I desperately wanted to get married and have a family. I attracted a great guy into my life but we had little in common with each other and didn't share the same goals or values and as I have mentioned earlier, that marriage didn't last. The end of my marriage was the beginning of an interesting period in my life – characterised by a few more failed relationships.

But I was saying all the right things, doing what I thought was necessary to attract the perfect relationship – I really wanted a relationship, I had so much to give, I was ready to commit … or was I?

It took me 14 years to realise that the reason I hadn't attracted the relationship of my dreams is that I had no real intention of letting myself be vulnerable to anyone. I was so scared of getting hurt, letting someone see the real me, risking loss or betrayal, trusting someone with my heart and depending on another. Yet that is precisely what I needed. I needed a real relationship where I was prepared to be vulnerable and risk everything – that was the only way I would truly heal. I wanted a lot but I was actually not willing to offer a great deal in return. Not because I didn't have anything to offer but because my primary intention was to protect and emotionally distance myself. More than anything I wanted to stay safe from hurt again – something that is almost impossible to do in the context of entering into an intimate relationship! My stated purpose was to find the relationship of a lifetime but I never truly intended to commit myself to another person. The realisation of this was particularly liberating.

I finally understood my true intention – I wanted to replace what I'd lost. In many ways the person wasn't important – essentially I wanted my family back. But the family is always or should always be secondary to a loving healthy relationship. My true intention was polluting my attempt to meet the right partner.

I have learnt that moving forward in life and making genuine progress demands a certain amount of self-assessment. I needed to understand myself more if I was ever to achieve the things I so desperately wanted. Initially, I started to keep a journal of thoughts and dreams and this process of introspection allowed me to read back and notice some recurring themes and patterns. But recognising the patterns and doing something to break free of them are two very different things.

Did you know ... ?

In a study in Stanford University a group of participants were asked to eat something particularly decadent. They were able to choose what that item was, for some it was a chocolate cake, for others cream cakes or donuts smothered in jam. It was found that regardless of the chosen treat, the thing that made the biggest difference was the intention given to that food. For example, those that ate the food while feeling guilt about how much damage they would be doing their bodies showed a dip in immune function. Those that ate without any reservations, remorse or worry showed a rise in immune function. The item of food made no immediate difference to the body other than the increase or decrease of the immune system; the change depended on the intent or meaning given to the experience, not the food itself.

As I have mentioned in previous chapters, my journey took me through what one might refer to as the 'traditional' therapies – medication, participation in victim support groups, counselling, retreats and group immersion forums. The bulk of the work done in these modalities was focused on talking about problems. Often in these environments healing is thought of as something that 'just takes time' – possibly years. In the early years I had a lot to say about what I felt and what I was experiencing and it helped to verbalise it and get things off my chest. Unfortunately, this endless talking about problems only served to further entrench my negative beliefs about myself.

I learned to suppress my feelings to the point that I could talk about the events of my life as if they had happened to someone else. I was so adept at this that I actually began to think that I had dealt with the underlying feelings. Really what I had done was literally 'push them down' into my lower gut (base chakra) where they slowly began to wreak havoc with my digestive system. If someone caught me off guard with an unexpected question, I felt like the façade slipped and I was completely exposed. Often my emotions would erupt uncontrollably, which left me feeling confused and extremely stressed. Talking about my problems was clearly not the answer.

I dabbled in all sorts of therapies where the treatment was directed at parts of my body such as my heart. I explored energetic healing and looking outside myself to others for answers. But nothing really worked for me until I engaged my mind. Although I began to appreciate how my experiences and the meaning that I attributed to those events were contributing metaphysically to both my health and my outward experience of life, I was still unable to make the changes necessary to propel me forward in a new and compelling direction. It felt like I was on the end of a bungee cord and I purposefully strode out toward my new future armed with my new insights but sooner or later the cord would stretch too far and I'd speed back to where I started. I just couldn't snap the cord and was constantly being pulled back to my past, regardless of the conscious knowledge I gathered.

It was only when I discovered the therapies that deal directly with the subconscious mind that I really began to make progress. I was drawn towards various sciences of the mind – NLP (neuro linguistic programming), hypnosis, Thought Field Therapy, psycho cybernetics and emotional intelligence. All of which allowed me to systematically work through incongruencies between what I said I wanted and what I unconsciously believed was possible. It was when I was able to harness their power that long-term healing and a happy fulfilling life became a real possibility for me.

In my experience, I have found the traditional therapies to be largely ineffective in sustaining long-term change because they fail to address the dominant unconscious factors. It's been said before but the analogy is perfect and therefore worth saying again. If you consider an iceberg – above the surface is a tiny peak that accounts for only 10% of the iceberg mass. Underneath is the 90% you can't see. The mind is exactly the same, the conscious mind is the tiny peak that appears above the surface and the subconscious mind is the powerhouse below. If you don't address that part of your mind, your long-term results will be sunk too. It is this part of your mind that provides context or meaning to the events in your life. It unwittingly influences the way you see yourself and this self-image then plays a large part in everything from your attitude, how you express yourself, what you believe is possible and the decisions you make.

You already have all of the answers and resources you need to heal yourself and achieve your dreams … They already exist in your own mind right now. There is nothing missing or broken or deficient – you just need to learn how re-connect to your dreams and the infinite resourcefulness of the subconscious mind via the courier of the self-image.

How to incorporate this wisdom into your life

Make a habit of getting to the root of your motivation. What is your 'why'? This applies to the interactions you have with others as surely as it applies to your dreams and aspirations. If, for example, you are not achieving the results you want in a particular area of your life – are you sure you understand your true motivation? Ask yourself why that is important to you? When you have an answer, ask why *that answer* is important to you and keep going until you find the truth.

The process can be extremely enlightening. If you stay with it and continue to question your own intention or reasons you will eventually arrive at a statement that may surprise you. Often in this process you will find yourself saying something – it will almost fall out your mouth without you realising what you've said and you will know in your heart that you've just spoken your truth. Being aware of these truths, even if they are surprising or uncomfortable is the first step toward aligning yourself to your chosen future.

Chapter 26

Ralph Waldo Emerson is widely regarded as one of the most influential authors, philosophers, orators and thinkers of the 19th century. He urged independent thinking and controversially stated that not all life's answers are found in books:' Books are the best of things, well used; abused, among the worst.' He believed that the best way to learn was by engaging fully in life.

The word 'obstacle' has got a bad rap. Even the mere sound of the word is quite ominous and foreboding. It is defined in the dictionary as 'a negative factor that hinders or prevents us from achieving our goals'. It strikes fear in the heart of many and seems to have developed the reputation for being a bad omen or a sign of impending failure.

Strangely enough, despite the bad press and menacing nature, everyone loves to focus on their obstacles. In fact, they seem to provide a welcome distraction. What do most people do when they encounter an obstacle? First, they may try to go around it. When that doesn't work, they pick it up and carry it around with them. They stop at nothing to show it to others, to talk about it and even ask us to carry it for them! Think about the last time you got together with friends, did the majority of the conversation focus on gratitude and celebration of recent successes or did the dialogue seem to gravitate towards the challenges and obstacles that everyone was experiencing?

Isn't that interesting?

Obstacles have a way of taking on a life of their own and they start to become the sole focus and obsession. They provide a handy excuse why we cannot do something or why 'it's just not meant to be'. The 'obstacle' is the consummate scapegoat – some see it as a 'sign' that they are simply not meant to achieve the goal … the problem, impediment or roadblock is just too big to be overcome by mere mortals.

But I'm going to let you in on a little secret … Obstacles are inherent in the process of setting goals – they don't exist until we plot a course for somewhere. If you have no goals or direction in life, then there can be no obstacles to contend with. If you have no destination then you can't possible meet obstacles on your journey toward nowhere. So the sure-fire way to eliminate obstacles forever is simply to wander aimlessly without any real purpose or direction. But that's not a very fulfilling way to live, is it? Without aspirations we would never feel that jubilation of success. Without dreams our life can drift along in a meaningless daze. We need to begin to think of and welcome obstacles as a sure sign that we are heading toward something worthwhile.

As a society we have developed a real apprehension about facing obstacles. Even though they are a natural part of the process of achievement, we have conditioned ourselves to believe that obstacles are threatening – a sign of impending failure or a validation for giving up. What if the 'obstacle' simply means that we are going somewhere, or that we are actually making progress towards achieving our goals? Would that simple shift in perspective and meaning change the way we feel about them and alter the foreboding influence they have over us?

By its very nature, language is extremely imprecise. We have an innate desire to give each word a definition – to increase the sense of security and certainty we have in our communication with others. But who determines how words are defined? After all, we have already established that the meaning we give to words has a huge impact on how they actually affect our state of mind and behaviours.

In my own life, it has never been the load or the obstacles that broke me, but rather the manner in which I chose to carry them. Never was this more apparent than when I decided that I wanted to become a permanent resident of Australia. I had already been living and working in Australia for about three years and I had been talking about applying for residency for most of that time. I finally decided in November 2006 that I would bite the bullet and commence the process. What should have been a three to four month endeavour turned into an eight-month marathon of paperwork and red tape.

It seemed like almost everything that could go wrong, did. I didn't bring copies of many of the documents that I needed and I was constantly on the phone or faxing Canada to obtain what was required. My status as a skilled migrant required verification by a governing body and this required extensive paperwork documenting my last five years of employment. The employer that sponsored me was not a normal 'corporation' – it was a joint venture of two large national businesses – and thus management was required to supply much more documentation and elaboration than would normally be required.

With every turn there was a new obstacle in my way. As I began to focus on and stress about the difficulties I also noticed that they began to multiply. The more I worried about the delays and setbacks, the more delays and setbacks I got. I was beginning to doubt whether the whole thing was actually worth the effort. Maybe the relentless obstacles were an indication that I wasn't meant to be here?

It was an enormous test of faith for me because it wasn't until I actually stepped back and literally got out of my own way that everything finally fell into place. As soon as I stopped complaining about the obstacles and instead focused on finding solutions to them I achieved my goal of permanent residency within a very short period of time. When I was able to view it from the other side and appreciate that the legislation was designed to ensure that those that applied to live in this wonderful country truly wanted it, then the obstacles even seemed sensible. I was being tested. Australia was testing me to make sure I really wanted this change and I was prepared to do whatever it took to achieve it. And I was also testing myself to see whether I would have the faith, perseverance and dedication to see it through.

Happily I passed the test. I had been on the right track all along. I had just spent most of my time battling the molehills instead of saving my energy for the mountain. I guess that is exactly what Al Neuharth meant when he said, '*The difference between a mountain and a molehill is your perspective*'.

Obstacles are merely a form of feedback – our way of knowing whether we are on or off course and allowing us the chance to make adjustments to get back on track. Oftentimes, the obstacle actually stands directly between us and our goals – thus, it is a very good sign that we are actually going in the right direction. By my estimation, the real cause for alarm should actually be raised when we do not encounter any obstacles at all! Perhaps that is a sign that we need to set some goals or are simply not progressing in the direction of our dreams?

If we can give a new meaning or definition to the obstacles that we face, we unlock the ability to face these opportunities head on and move through them quickly and easily. Obstacles are just part of life, welcome them as reminders that you are alive and vibrant and able to surmount anything in your path. Obstacles prove we are on the right track. Learn to 'get out of our own way' and you will see that you can conquer even your biggest fears.

Did you know ... ?

Cybernetics is the science of control. The word cybernetic was appropriately suggested by Norbert Weiner (1894-1964), a mathematician who refined guided missile technology, and it comes from the Greek word for 'steersman'. Cybernetic usually refers to the study and design of devices for maintaining stability, for homing-in on a particular goal or target.

Maxwell Maltz, the author of *Psycho Cybernetics*, coined the word 'psycho-cybernetics'. It essentially bridges the divide between the traditional mechanistic models of brain functioning and the knowledge that man is much more than simply a 'machine'. Maltz surmised that the constant feedback loop that enables a guided missile to maintain direction and stay on course could also be applied to human achievement.

The key point is that cybernetics looks at systems where actions are influenced by feedback received from the results of prior actions. In other words, we can learn by our mistakes, or learn as we go.

Let's say that you've set a goal, made some efforts to reach it and encountered some obstacles along the way. Cybernetics says that you can review your efforts to date and change your game plan. Rarely do we reach a goal by a direct and obstacle free path. Instead the obstacles and challenges act like negative feedback to correct your heading and re-focus you in the direction of your goal. It has been said that on a flight between Sydney and Los Angeles, an aeroplane is only directly on course for less than 5% of the trip. Most of the time, the plane is actually slightly off course and the feedback mechanism of the plane's computer is constantly making slight course corrections to direct the plane toward its ultimate destination.

Essentially the plane zigzags back and forth as it moves toward the target. Out brain does the same thing – locked on a target but correcting and adjusting the route as and when obstacles appear. Maxwell Maltz believed that we are natural goal setters and goal achievers and that our physical brain and nervous system form a kind of machine – a 'servo-mechanism'. In our conscious mind we decide to set a goal. Once we set a goal, our subconscious mind will guide us to that destination – acting like a guided missile or a plane on autopilot.

In the same way that a guided missile or plane uses 'sense organs' (radar, sonar, heat receptors, computer programs etc) to bring information from the target and correct its course, the human brain responds to feedback from obstacles sensed by the nervous system whenever you perform any purposeful activity – even in simple goal-seeking situations like picking up a book from a table, learning to drive or studying a foreign language.

As humans, we are able to accomplish goals because of a similar automatic mechanism, and not by 'will' and forebrain thinking alone. All that the forebrain does is to select the goal, trigger it into action by desire, and feed information to the automatic mechanism so that your course is continually corrected. In fact, most of the time, you are really off course. The obstacles that you encounter provide feedback to get you back on track. That means they are a blessing and not a curse!

How to incorporate this wisdom into your life

Take a look around your life right now – do you see obstacles and adversity? Write down the top five obstacles that you are currently facing in your life. Taking each in turn, how else could you view this situation? Is it possible that delays are not denials but a chance for you to fine tune your approach and make yourself stronger and the result better? Try to look at your challenges from another perspective. For example, in my situation, I was able to see that the delays I faced in gaining residency were a logical and vital step to ensure that only the most dedicated people were allowed permanent entry to the country.

Assess each obstacle and for each one find at least one alternative perspective. Also come up with at least one new solution. Obstacles can offer us new insight or enhance our resolve – they are never there to stop us dead in our tracks. They are speed bumps not brick walls. The secret is to dig deep and find a way to surmount your challenge by confronting it head on and to feel the elation of success in the journey toward your goal as well as your ultimate arrival at that destination.

Get wildly excited about your obstacles because they demonstrate that you are exactly where you need to be. Look out into the distance past the challenge and you will see your prize – your goal. Never take your eyes of the prize – especially not for an insignificant little thing like an obstacle.

Chapter 27

Live out of your imagination, not your history' ~ Stephen R Covey

Stephen R Covey wrote the best-selling book, The Seven Habits of Highly Effective People – which has sold over 15 million copies worldwide. Covey argues that values govern people's behaviour, but principles ultimately determine the consequences. Covey presents his teachings in a series of habits, manifesting as a progression from dependence via independence to interdependence. He is a proud father of nine and a grandfather of 47 and recently received the Fatherhood Award from the [American] National Fatherhood Initiative.

WARNING: Past performance does not guarantee future results.

If I had a dollar for every time I saw that legal caveat I'd be an extremely rich woman. It's used everywhere from investment seminars, weight reduction programs, multi-level marketing schemes to quit smoking products. Someone wants to sell you their services or product but almost no one is willing to put themselves on the line and actually guarantee the results. Why is that? What is so different about the future? Why is it not reasonable to expect exactly the same results that were obtained in the past?

To me this is an interesting dichotomy – why are we so quick to accept that the past does not equal the future when we are purchasing something yet that same principle does not seem to govern other areas of our lives? Isn't the very reason why we have sought help with our finances, looked into how we can lose weight and get into shape because we are worried that if we don't do something the past *will* equal the future?

Just because you have stayed in a job, relationship or situation where you are unhappy for 15 years does not mean that you must continue to stay there. If you do stay, however, then you can't reasonably expect a different result. The key to moving forward is as simple as acknowledging and accepting the past is in the past and making new decisions *now* to move forward towards your new and compelling future. The past is the past. Yet, why do so many of us continue to live by rules and choices made years ago?

One possible explanation for our continued urge to do what doesn't work is 'consistency'. In his astonishing book *Influence Science and Practice,* Robert B Cialdini talks of the six basic yet extremely powerful principles of psychology that direct human behaviour. They are:

o   Reciprocation (the feeling of obligation to repay favours, gifts, invitations etc)
o   Consistency (the need to remain consistent with earlier choices)
o   Social Proof (the need to check what others like you are doing in order to work out whether a behaviour is acceptable or not)
o   Liking (we do more for people we like)
o   Authority (the need to need authority)
o   Scarcity (often used by marketers to make us think a product is scarce. The risk of missing out will propel people to action.)

Consistency relates to the innate need to remain consistent in our choices and behaviours. If you stay in an abusive relationship, for example, the longer you stay the more compelled you are to continue to stay because it validates your initial decision. Human beings want to be right. We have an almost obsessive desire to be and appear to be consistent with what we have already done. Once we make a choice or take a stand we are innately drawn to things that galvanise, justify and validate that position. The force is so strong that it will often compel us toward action or inaction that is clearly not in our best interest.

There is also the issue of conditioned responses and the existence of neural pathways that allow us to bypass conscious thought and slip straight into habit! So granted, there are some strong forces being brought to bear to repeat the past.

But understanding that and deliberately making new choices can break those patterns. The past only equals the future if you allow it to be through non-engagement with your own life. Life is not a passive activity – get involved and make real choices for your life.

We can all allow the past to influence our future and it's logical that it would. We are learning creatures. As a child we learn not to touch a stove by touching a stove. But the same doesn't necessarily apply as adults

Did you know ... ?

The thing that makes us different from all other animals is the ratio of frontal lobe to the rest of the brain. The frontal lobe is the home of firm intention, decision-making, regulating behaviour and inspiration. It is this part of the brain that gives us the power of choice and allows us to scan the environment and make new decisions. Without the frontal lobe we would automatically repeat the past through conditioned responses.

Unless we consciously engage the frontal lobe we are destined to repeat the past because it has been proven the nerve cells that fire together wire together. If you practice something over and over again then those nerve cells create a long-term relationship – a neural pathway or 'super highway' in your brain. This relationship allows you to duplicate a result very quickly if given the correct stimuli. This can work for the positive such as learning how to play the piano or it can work for the negative such as being angry every day. The frontal lobe gives us free will. It is up to us to exercise that and learn to assess each situation afresh instead of automatically reacting to the external stimuli. If we continue to use automatic responses that are already wired in our brain as a result of past situations and known results, then we are not exercising our free will and we will continue to get what we have always got.

The frontal lobe allows us to break those patterns. Just as practice strengthens those connections lack of use diminishes them. So by breaking the patterns of your behaviour and doing new things and thinking new thoughts you can re-structure your brain to create new tomorrows.

Just by reading this book and opening your mind to new perspectives, you are literally creating new neural pathways and that's exciting!

where we have great cognitive ability to make reasoned, logical choices. I know, for example, that I can touch a stove if I wear oven gloves. I also know that if I touch a stove by accident it won't kill me and running my hand under cold water will help. I have more information now!

It's natural to be apprehensive of your future when you relate it to similar past experiences that didn't pan out. You might be reluctant to start a new business because your last one failed or you might be wary of getting married for a second time because you were badly hurt in your first marriage. You might be terrified of speaking in public because the last time you did it you wet your pants. The fact that you were nine years old doesn't seem to diminish your fear, even though it should!

If you take only one concept and apply it in your life, I would like it to be this one. This principle alone will set you free. All of us have had things happen in the past, which we hope will never happen again. However, all too often these experiences are being used as excuses to legitimise your inactivity right now!

I turned 40 last year. I wasn't particularly bothered about the age milestone but it definitely made me look back on my life and reflect about where I was and what I was doing. I have had a dream for a long time to write this book – to share my stories and experiences with others in a way that would inspire and empower them come to their own edge and fly! I saw myself speaking in front of large audiences, influencing change in organisations and helping individuals to live their dreams by unleashing the limitless resources of their subconscious minds. But yet I held back. I was in a very good place with my career and felt reluctant to let go of the security and certainty of a sizeable salary. But more importantly, I was afraid to fail. I had, after all, already had my own business before and it didn't work.

My retail clothing business From Here to Maternity had initially gone well and I even won some awards for it. Unfortunately the time I needed funding to expand coincided with the tragedy of September 11, 2001. That event had a profound impact on the capital markets internationally and severely restricted the availability of investment funds for projects like mine. At the same time, my marriage of seven years ended and we were forced to divide up the assets – including our home, which was the main piece of collateral on the business loan.

Those two simultaneous losses were a huge blow for me. I lost my partner in life (and his family) and I lost my business and the ability to support myself. The collapse of the business had significant financial ramifications for both my ex and I. I was pretty much wiped out. I was 34 years old – divorced, unemployed, emotionally exhausted and beating myself up about it.

The memory of that failure and my fear around it recurring were the single biggest reason why it took me so long to start my new business, Imagineering Unlimited.

The difference that made the difference for me was a conversation with a close friend of mine, Debra Tate. She asked me to describe the business that I had in Canada and list the reasons why it failed. She then asked me to describe what my new business would be like and specifically how it would be different from the one that failed.

I was immediately able to see there were quite a few differences between the business that I had in the past and the new venture that I wanted to start. She then said to me, *'On a scale from 1 to 100, how responsible were you for the failure of the business in Canada?'* *'That's easy'*, I said, *'100%. I owned it and I have no one else to blame'.*

She then said, *'What about your divorce? On a scale from 1 to 100, how responsible were you?'* After some reflection I replied, *'To be fair, I think we were each 50% responsible.'*

Debra then asked me what I learnt from each situation. When I'd finished describing what I had learnt she leaned into me and said, *'That's really interesting. You were 50% responsible for your divorce, got some really valuable lessons and are now open and willing to take a chance a second time. Since you were actually 100% responsible for your business, isn't it possible that you actually got twice the learnings?'*

In that moment, the penny really dropped for me. I had never looked at it that way – I just assumed that if I were 100% responsible it must mean that it was more of a liability, not more of an asset through the insights I gained. Not only did I finally grasp that the past does not equal the future but I realised that I could set myself free from the fear and shame of my past failures and focus 100% of my energy on my future and my new dreams. This simple statement helped me to remove a limiting belief that I had about my ability to start and run a successful business. I started my business and this book two days later and I have not looked back.

Every night when you arrive home from work, you go into your refrigerator or cupboards to find ingredients to prepare your dinner. You would never think of going through the garbage can to find produce, staples and condiments for your meal. Then it begs the question – why would you look to your past failures, essentially the garbage can of your mind, to decide what you are capable of in the future? There are no helpful resources or suggestions there, only the past and reasons why you will not succeed. As Dr Wayne Dyer correctly points out, *'I liken the past to the wake of a boat. It does not drive the boat nor does it determine the direction it is headed. It only shows where it has been'.*

It's unrealistic to expect we will approach all new situations in life with the benefit of a stellar track record of success. Setbacks and failures occur – they are part of the learning process. Nothing was ever invented or created by people who were afraid to try because they had previously failed at some endeavour. Look at any successful person from history and you will find a person who continued to try and who refused to believe that their past would foreshadow their destiny. Your biography does not pre-determine your destiny – your past has absolutely no bearing on your future but if you continue to do what you have always done then you will get what you've always got!

How to incorporate this wisdom into your life

Buy two small plastic garbage bins – one for work and one for home. Write 'the past does not equal the future' on the garbage bins with an indelible marker. Start to pay attention to what you say – either aloud or to yourself. If possible, enlist the support of friends and family to help you keep yourself accountable. Each time you catch yourself limiting what you can do in the future, based on constraints and failures from the past, write down the phrase and put it the garbage together with $1.

Take an inventory at the end of each week. Do certain specific limitations seem to be coming up over and over again? Are there particular areas of your life where you are not achieving the results that you want? Is it possible that these limiting beliefs are contributing to that in some way? What new meaning do you need to give your past so as to release you to move forward?

You will know when you no longer need to monitor these limiting statements – you will begin to get different results in your life. To reward yourself use the money you have collected in the bins to treat yourself or support a cause that is close to your heart.

Chapter 28

*If we could read the secret history of our enemies, we would find
in each person's life sorrow and suffering enough to disarm
all hostility. ~ Henry Wadsworth Longfellow*

Henry Wadsworth Longfellow (1807-1882) is probably the best loved of American poets and storytellers the world over. A number of his famous phrases have become familiar to us as rhymes from Mother Goose or the words of nursery songs learned in childhood. Despite his father's intentions for him to become a lawyer, Longfellow knew instinctively that he was born to put pen to paper and he famously wrote to his father 'The fact is, I most eagerly aspire after future eminence in literature; my whole soul burns most ardently for it, and every earthly thought centers in it … .' He married twice over the course of his lifetime and lost both wives under tragic circumstances – one to illness and the other to a fire.

The word *forgive* is translated from the Latin word *'perdonare'* which means to give completely without reservation, or completely give. In Greek, *forgiveness* is the same word as release or letting go. Both of these definitions conjure up sensations of liberation, capitulation and freedom. On paper, it reads like a natural and benevolent process – something one freely GIVES to another to release yourself and others from the past. In practice, it is often misunderstood as something that someone who has done us wrong must ASK of us.

The most precious gift that we have is our breath – without it, we would simply die. We can live for a short time without food, water, love and light but we cannot live for more than a minute or two without air. Breathing in and exhaling signifies the natural inevitability of the cycle of life: We take into our bodies the oxygen we need to live and we release or let go of carbon dioxide and other by-products that no longer serve us.

Our experience of life bears a striking resemblance to this natural process. We are constantly taking in the world around us and our interactions with others produce a myriad of consequences – some are positive while others are not. Unfortunately, negative or hurtful experiences are inevitable. As human beings we all have the same capacity to inflict harm through our words, actions and inactions, whether knowingly or unknowingly. But we all know that we cannot hold our breath forever; the release of by products and things that no longer serve us is an instinctive function. By the same token, sooner or later we all must discover our innate capacity to forgive.

Forgiveness, like exhaling, is an act of faith. It can neither be stopped nor compelled. There is no proof that peace will follow or that the release from anger, vengeance or self-righteousness will be immediate.

When my mother first passed away, I was understandably incredibly angry. I always said that if the police hadn't already arrested the kids who were responsible, I would have probably killed them myself with my bare hands. Surprisingly, as the shock and grief subsided over time, my anger actually grew. I was mad at the whole world and angry with God for taking her away from me. I resented that everyone around me was getting on with their lives and I was furious that two of the culprits only received sentences of three years in prison for conspiracy to commit first-degree murder because they were only 16 years old. Their age didn't stop them killing my Mom why should it stop them paying for it? How could taking the life of an incredible woman, someone who had so much to offer and who made such an amazing contribution, be worth just three years? Some criminals go to jail for longer after committing minor property offences. They would be out and free to live their lives in only three years and I had been given the life sentence.

I also struggled to come to grips with the fact that my grandparents had chosen to forgive the four perpetrators almost immediately. My grandparents had very strong religious convictions and they felt it was imperative to forgive as soon as possible. They had brought me up to believe in God and to do what was right but I just couldn't. The more they insisted and pressured, the more I resisted. I simply wasn't ready – the fact that the perpetrators showed no signs of remorse seemed to galvanise my determination to keep them on the hook emotionally. Perhaps what they realised quicker than I did is that forgiveness is not about letting someone off the hook or allowing them to escape proper accountability but that forgiveness is the ultimate gift of self-acceptance and love. It is essentially choosing not to hurt yourself anymore over things that cannot be changed. By forgiving others you also forgive yourself and that is what is liberating.

But at the time I did not see that. I had very little emotional support because my father felt obligated to come to the defence of my brother. For a lot of reasons, I think he felt morally culpable for what happened. Violence begets violence and we had grown up in a home where alcoholism, threats and abuse were normal. He had also directed a great deal of hatred toward my mother after the divorce and my brother bought into that perspective. In many ways it's no surprise that it ended as it did. I always knew that someone was going to get hurt, I just never knew that someone was going to die.

Of all the chapters in this book, I struggled with writing this one the most. It took me six years to forgive my brother and the other boys that were involved. I will never understand why they did it but I have chosen to accept that perhaps they all had a secret history full of sorrow and suffering.

In the case of my brother, I witnessed his distress and anguish first hand. As a young boy he would sit on his bed and cry – too many times my Dad had promised that he would come to visit and simply not shown up. There was always an excuse but for the most part we knew that he was at the bar drinking with his buddies. There was always someone or something that was more important than the promises he made to us.

There were many times that he forgot our birthdays and Christmas – my Mom covered it up by buying and wrapping presents that she said were from him. Then there were the phone calls and letters – where he told my brother that it was my Mom's fault that he had to go away and we could not be a family any more. I knew better. I was six years older and I had heard the fights – where he came home drunk, told her that he hated her and threatened to kill us all.

I will never forget the day that I drove to the jail to face my brother. It had been six years since Mom had died and I had heard that he might get early parole. I was overwhelmed by fear and anxiety about the thought of possibly running into him on the street. I had been journaling and praying everyday for about a year to find the strength and peace to forgive him and let this go. When I found out about his impending parole, I made the decision then and there to forgive him and to do it face-to-face.

It was the longest one-and-a-half hour drive of my life. I watched every street sign, lamppost, fence and building along that stretch of highway as if it were to be the last that I would ever see. So many thoughts and emotions were flashing through my mind. I played and re-played what I would say over and over again in my head. It all seemed so clinical; an esoteric, methodical exercise. The actual meeting couldn't have been further from that. I remember the first time that I set eyes on him – he looked so small, withdrawn and helpless. I'm not even sure if I would have recognised him if we had bumped into each other on the street. Neither one of us said very much. I tried. I had the whole thing planned out and rehearsed in my mind. But the only thing that I could do was cry. I cried for the fact that she had suffered so much. I cried for the loss and the closure that I had in finally realising on that day that she was never coming back. I cried for fact that I hadn't spoken to my brother or my father in six years.

In my head I had worked him up to be some sort of monster. In reality, all I saw in front of me that day was the scared little boy who sat on his bed wondering why his daddy went away and didn't show up on his birthday. I felt my anger and outrage instantly melt away and underneath I discovered an ocean of tears and grief. It was only then that I was able to begin the process of healing. I had spent six years punishing myself and everyone else for something that simply could not be undone. Once I had made the initial decision that I actually wanted to forgive, ironically I had already done about 70% of the actual work. The rest came relatively easily and naturally. The most difficult part is making the decision that you want to forgive.

The day when I actually saw him, I knew that I had forgiven him because the anger and resentment slipped away and my true emotions of bottomless pain and loss emerged. I was heartbroken. I suddenly realised that forgiveness was not the end of the healing process, it was the start! The anger I felt and the refusal to forgive was nothing more than a band-aid solution because I couldn't bear to feel the hurt and betrayal underneath. When I saw my brother that band-aid fell off and I was immersed in those core emotions. Accessing that truth allowed me to face them honestly, feel the pain and find a way to deal with it. It wasn't necessary for me to hold him accountable for my pain anymore, besides it was quite clear he was suffering, fighting his own demons.

The same is also true of my father, although I do still struggle at times. I've also come to understand that forgiveness isn't a one-off event; it's an ongoing evolving process. And some days I'm further along that process than others. I think part of that is because he is my father. Fathers are supposed to protect and nurture their kids, be there for them and support them through difficult times and yet he never did. I don't feel as though he ever took responsibility for anything that happened in our lives and there is no doubt in my mind that his venom toward my Mom is the reason she is no longer with us.

But I am a work in progress and there are still days I find it difficult to believe that this happened in my life. But I am sure that one day I will forgive him completely. I don't know if we will ever have a meaningful relationship but I will find a way to lay this to rest. As Beverly Flanagan, author of *Forgiving the Unforgivable – Overcoming the Legacy of Intimate Wounds*, so rightly points out, '*In a way, forgiving is only for the brave. It is for people, who are willing to confront their pain, accept themselves as permanently changed and make different choices. Countless individuals are satisfied to go on resenting and hating people that have wronged them. They stew in their own inner poisons and contaminate those around them. Forgivers, on the other hand, are not content to be stuck in a quagmire. They reject the possibility that the rest of their lives will be determined by the unjust and injurious actions of another person*'.

I don't want to stew in any inner poison. As Honore De Blazac says, '*The heart of a mother is a deep abyss at the bottom of which you will always find forgiveness*'. I know my Mom would want me to forgive completely and move on. And for the most part I have done that but I still have a little way to go.

It has been suggested by many that we never really completely understand life until we face death – that we cannot fully comprehend the bigger picture until we are confronted with the certainty of death. What if we all started off on our deathbeds? Would it make a difference? Would it change the way we choose to play the game? Would it take us to forgiveness sooner?

On our deathbed, I doubt any of us would say 'I wish I held onto more anger and resentment or took a bit longer to forgive.' In fact, if you were to look out into the future and imagine the world and all of your relationships from a position where you knew with absolute certainty that they would be gone tomorrow, would you act differently today?

Would you regret not having closure? Would you mourn the years that you kept yourself enslaved by bitterness, blame and indignation? Would you lament the loss of pleasure, love and peace that could have been yours if only you could have found a way to forgive sooner? Does the thing that you are fighting or obsessing about now really even matter?

Forgiveness is often thought of as the domain of religion. Perhaps that is why so many of us resist and rebel against this very natural and innate process? We feel it is something that someone else is telling us we must do, rather than seeing it as an integral, natural and inherent part of life. Regardless of our faith, we are taught that it is mandated to 'forgive and forget'. We are scolded and chastised by elders when we do not let go, yet we see evidence all around us of our role models carrying hurts and grudges of various sizes for years, if not decades. As with most things, we pay attention to what they do and not to what they say.

In the process of relegating forgiveness solely to the domain of religion, we have essentially done ourselves a huge disservice. In the discerning words of Tian Dayton, author of *The Magic of Forgiveness, 'we send our bodies to the doctor, our minds to school, our emotions to therapists and our souls to religious institutions'*. Our ability to forgive affects much more than just our souls. It has already been scientifically proven that what we think and feel shows up in our physical bodies and also influences everything from our emotional well being to how we live and die.

Forgiveness is never easy but it is necessary – necessary to unlock us from a vicious, self-deprecating cycle of recrimination, anger, righteousness and revenge. None of us are perfect and as such we are all destined to experience both – the need to forgive and the desire to be forgiven. Perhaps that is why Longfellow's quote is so moving? For it is precisely at the time that we are being called upon to release and let go that we are reminded to have compassion for the sorrow and suffering of our enemies.

We all know our own pain – we are intimately familiar with the injustices that we have suffered, the crosses we have had to bear and the countless nights that we have cried ourselves to sleep. What we don't fully grasp is the depth of another's pain – the unspoken abuse, neglect, prejudices, anguish, loss, torment or afflictions. At the time, we think we are the only ones who are hurting and we forget that the scars and burdens of others are not always visible on the outside. We can never truly know another's plight until we have walked a mile in their shoes. As I said above, the first step toward forgiveness is simply the willingness to take one's own shoes off and put another's on. The rest can be surprisingly easy.

Did you know ... ?

The connection between emotion and health was first recorded over 2000 years ago by Galen when he observed that women with a depressed nature were more prone to cancer than cheerful women. Evidence to support this hypothesis has grown ever since. The most compelling of which was a consolidation of 101 smaller studies by Friedman & Boothby-Kewley. The study confirmed that negative emotions such as anger, resentment, hostility and sadness, the hallmarks of those unable to forgive, were found to double the risk of disease including asthma, arthritis and heart disease.

The inner poison mentioned by Beverly Flanagan is not metaphorical, it's real. The emotions we experience because of the resentment and pain that we direct at another person actually create a toxic environment for our own body which begs the question, 'Who is really suffering from your inability to forgive?' You and only you!

How to incorporate this wisdom into your life

The struggle with forgiveness is that it implies that we are saying to someone, 'It's okay what you did.' But that is not what forgiveness is all about. You can forgive someone without validating or excusing their actions. Forgiveness is about freeing yourself from the past so you can move forward into your future without poisoning your life.

There is no easy way to do this so I won't profess to have a simple exercise that will miraculously cure you of your anger and resentment. First, you merely must make a conscious choice to let go. Wanting to forgive is 70% of the battle.

Try to ascertain if there is anything in the other person's life that you would feel compassion for? Perhaps if you were able to see that person as the scared little child, you could begin to see that we are all doing the best we can with the resources that we think we have available at the time? Maybe this person entered into a spiritual contract with you to hurt you in this way so that you might grow and evolve spiritually? If you need to, go back to Chapter 21 and revisit the story 'The Little Soul in the Sun'. Find a way to let go – whatever works for you. Most of all, you owe it to yourself.

Chapter 29

You'll see it when you believe it ~ Wayne Dyer

Wayne W Dyer PhD is an internationally renowned author and speaker in the field of self-development. He's the author of 30 books, has created many audio programs and has appeared on thousands of television and radio shows. Dr Wayne Dyer is affectionately called the 'father of motivation' by his fans. Despite a childhood spent in orphanages and foster homes, Dr Dyer has overcome many obstacles to make his dreams come true. Today he spends his time and energy showing others how to do the same.

To me this quote points to the need for faith. Not in a religious context but simply the ability to believe in something regardless of any demonstration of proof. So often we will have heard the comment, 'I will believe it when I see it.' This 'prove it to me first' mentality is the domain of Western culture. And yet Dyer's quote is particularly intriguing because it is the exact antithesis of everything that we have been led to believe. There are things in life that we will never prove. Religion is built on a theory that is ostensibly impossible to prove and yet religion provides comfort to billions of people around the world. So much so that even if proof was found that indicated none of it was true, people would still believe.

What if we could transfer that certainty and belief to ourselves? What if we could learn to believe in our own ability and possibility regardless of whether any past proof exists? Wayne Dyer reminds us that this sort of thinking is imperative if we are ever to transform our lives for the better. We have to believe that it is possible BEFORE it can ever come into physical reality.

All things begin in the mind. Everything you see around you in terms of inventions and modern comforts begin first as a single isolated thought in someone's mind. That person believed strongly enough in the unknown to continue with the planning and development until finally it made it into the physical reality.

What we are really talking about here is certainty – a complete confidence or faith in something regardless of whether any evidence exists regarding its feasibility. When *we* get certain, that is when certainty will manifest around us. And yet certainty seems to have a mercurial quality. We live in an uncertain world where it is difficult to know what will happen from one moment to the next. Each day we are confronted with all manner of bad news that shakes our confidence and rocks our certainty. Terrorism, disease, tragedy, injustice, technological glitches and natural disasters all work against us to have certainty slip from our grasp once again.

This need for certainty is one of the strongest of our core needs – and it is common to all people. Regardless of sex, race, religion, culture or background, humans will often choose certainty over almost everything else. The known offers comfort and safety so it's hardly surprising it's so attractive to us. For most of us this means that we will avoid what we don't know or understand. When we do not have enough certainty in our world, we can struggle to function. At the very core of our being, certainty often equates to survival in our minds.

So how do we create certainty in our lives? Although we all share the same need we have different strategies to illicit certainty – some are negative while others are positive. You may choose to do something – threaten to leave, use violence, bury yourself in your work or detach emotionally – to get a sense of control over the situation or others. Some may use cigarettes, food or money to make themselves feel more certain or comfortable. While others may create a negative identity for themselves to give the illusion of consistency or predictability – 'I'm unlucky, bad things always happen to me, so losing my job is no surprise.' We may even go so far as to sacrifice another core need like love and connection or significance to ensure we feel certainty. Think of the person who stays in an abusive relationship. Their need for certainty can override all other needs.

Ironically, it is in these types of moments that Wayne Dyers quote is so important. Within each of us is a wellspring of faith and certainty. It may have been decades since you experienced it but it is always there. We have all the resources we will ever need to make changes and create the life we truly desire. There is a system inside us that if we just believe it to be possible and have faith in ourselves, the possibilities are infinite. But you have to believe it before you can ever tap into it. And therein lies the rub …

Regardless of which strategies you consistently employ to gain certainty, they are all just habits. To succeed, you need to expand your epistemology, which is the scope of the habits you have to choose from. When you acknowledge uncertainty but act positively anyway, you lose both your fear and the need to have certainty at all costs. Or as Anthony Robbins puts it, *'Do what you fear and the death of fear is certain'*. The more certain YOU are inside and the more you expand your epistemology, the more successful you will become at managing your life.

Think about it, if you are going to be a highly successful person, chances are you will almost always be operating in areas where you do not know exactly what you are doing. Pablo Picasso famously once remarked, *'I am always doing things I can't do, that's how I get to do them'*. And he would know, he created some of the most famous, memorable and unique works of art and sculpture that the world has ever seen. In order to succeed and progress in anything, Picasso recognised the need to create certainty out of uncertainty. He had faith in himself and no matter what situation he found himself in, he knew in his heart that he had the ability and resources to work out a solution.

If you live in your comfort zone where things are already certain, you will never get ahead or learn anything new. If you never learn anything new your brain chemistry won't change and you'll continue to repeat old patterns. The extent to which you can aspire to reach great heights and results in every area of your life is directly proportionate to the amount of uncertainty that you can cope with in those areas.

Interestingly enough, the biggest decisions that we make in life, more often than not, follow events that we cannot possibly prepare for or anticipate. The love of your life is killed in an accident, you lose your job right before Christmas, a loved one gets diagnosed with an incurable disease, your spouse is transferred to another city by his or her employer, you find out that you are pregnant or you lose $100,000 on the stock market. By their nature, these events create a level of uncertainty that is opportunistically uncomfortable. At this moment, change and growth are not only imminent but also inevitable. These life-changing moments will happen regardless of whether we try to control them or not.

True certainty has less to do with outside events and more to do with who we are on the inside. No one can take certainty away from you: You can only take it away from yourself by the questions you ask yourself and the habits you rely on to cope. If you keep asking the wrong questions or repeating negative habits you actually create more uncertainty or doubt and you will never have the life of your dreams.

Did you know ... ?

We can see this phenomenon playing out in various indigenous cultures. The power of voodoo, for example, is widely attributed in nothing more than a certainty that 'pointing the bone,' means death. It is the mental certainty that accounts for the following illness or death not necessarily any mystical power shown by the medicine man.

We have all had times when we were faced with massive uncertainty, where we felt overwhelmed, out of control and scared. I can still remember vividly the day that I found out my mother had been murdered – I was in a state of complete shock and I wasn't even sure that I was physically going to make it through the night. Initially, I created a negative identity for myself, as a victim, to create a sense of consistency and certainty in my world. Ironically, as time progressed, I began to notice that this habit didn't really create any more certainty and it certainly didn't get me the results that I wanted. Something had to change and that something wasn't on the 'outside'.

What eventually pulled me through was a deep sense within me that I had made it through the worst. With that knowledge came an understanding that if I could get through that, there was nothing that I could not face. I realised that I desperately needed to expand the habits I had formed, get access to better information, start asking myself more resourceful questions and to find faith in something bigger than just what I could see with my eyes. I found the quote by Richard Nixon in Chapter 1, *'The strongest steel goes through the hottest fire'* and I adopted it as part of my new, positive identity. The day I finally believed that I was made of the strongest steel was the day that I looked in the mirror and saw a reflection of a survivor and someone who could genuinely help others find their way out of difficult times. My experiences gave me a unique insight to what the worst of life is really like and how it is possible to find a way out of the darkness.

Once I discovered how to create certainty out of uncertainty, it opened up a whole world of opportunity. Shortly thereafter, I tackled one of my biggest fears and I learned to swim … at the age of 28! As a young child, I had several negative experiences and I was absolutely terrified of going into water that was over my head. The uncertainty of not being able to touch or see the bottom frightened me and it was easier for me to walk away or make excuses than face the fear head on. As a result, I missed out on a lot of opportunities to spend time with my friends in the pool or at the lake because of my need to have absolute certainty in this area of my life.

When I finally let go of that need, I discovered that not only was I a pretty decent swimmer, I actually loved being in the water. I now enjoy swimming, sailing, snorkelling and even scuba diving. I essentially missed out on doing something (which I love) for 28 years because I needed to 'see it before I believed it'. I needed to know I would be okay before I would take a chance. But life doesn't work that way – you have to take the chance first. Besides as someone once said, *'If you aren't in over your head, how do you know how tall you are?'*

How to incorporate this wisdom into your life

One of the simplest and most powerful ways to alter the beliefs you hold about yourself and what's possible is through hypnosis. A skilled hypnotherapist will be able to brush the conscious mind aside and get straight into the subconscious beliefs, emotions, attitudes and values that could be holding you back.

Maxwell Maltz of *Psycho Cybernetics* realised that despite his skill as a plastic surgeon some of his patients didn't see the improvements. Their internal 'self-image' was not altered even though their outside disfigurement was. Dr Maltz went on to create psycho-cybernetics to reverse that process so that they could create a positive self imagine regardless of any external features of events.

On some level, you and I have attracted everything we are or have into our lives based on our self-image to date. No amount of conscious direction will affect our results if our unconscious self-image is negative or destructive. Repeating 'I am rich' 10,000 times a day will not make an iota of difference if your self-image believes you will always be poor. You have to re-create the subconscious self-image to match your conscious choices and imagining it vividly in the theatre of your mind does just that. When the conscious and subconscious mind are in congruent alignment, miracles will happen . This is the essence of the science of psycho-cybernetics and the basis upon which I have developed the techniques that I use with my clients to achieve lasting changes and results.

Chapter 30

Character is what you are in the dark. ~ Dwight L Moody

> Dwight Lyman Moody was an American evangelist who founded the Moody Church. He is touted as being the greatest evangelist of the 19th century attracting crowds of up to 30,000. One of nine children, his mother struggled to raise them after their alcoholic father died at 41. Despite the hardship they all faced, his mother continued to send them all to church. Moody was also the founder of a number of schools, the Moody Bible Institute and Moody Publishers.

I have experienced some dark moments in my life and if character is illustrated in those moments then I can't help but see the stark contrast of character that was illustrated in the court case against my brother and the other perpetrators. I was torn between doing the right thing – telling the truth about what I knew and witnessed in the months before she died – and not wanting to testify against him. My father was so angry with me – he felt that if I did testify, my brother would surely go to jail. He felt compelled to support him and to do what he could to prevent him from going to jail and hired a very well known defense lawyer to ensure that he got a fair trial. He called me right before my mother's funeral to insist that I didn't testify. He didn't plead with me in desperation, he didn't explain how difficult the situation was for him, torn between two children he loved, he didn't tell me how responsible he felt or how sorry he was that it had happened, he didn't tell me about any remorse my brother felt. Instead he got aggressive and told me in no uncertain terms that if I did testify and he went to jail, it would be my fault!

I was devastated. It was the last conversation we had for over ten years. I felt completely betrayed and I realised in that moment that I was totally alone. I missed my mother, my brother was in jail, I was distraught at having to testify against him and I felt that my father had effectively turned his back on me. It was by far the lowest point; I had lost my entire family.

I didn't want to be part of sending my brother to jail but at the same time I had to do the right thing and defend my Mom. Justice had to be served – I owed her that.

Nothing that I had ever done before could have prepared me for testifying in open court. I was absolutely terrified and overwhelmed with emotions. The courtroom was packed with spectators, police and the media – I felt as though everyone's eyes were on me, scrutinising my every word.

I have never felt terror like it before or since. My knees were shaking so badly that I could barely walk to the stand. I was hyperventilating – I felt nauseous and I struggled to get every word out. I couldn't even look in the vague direction of my brother. When asked to point him out I just motioned in the general direction. I tried to fix my gaze on the Crown Prosecutor, Darwin Greaves. He was someone that I trusted and knew I could depend on. He helped me through it – he knew exactly what he had to do to keep me safe and to get me off the stand and out of the courtroom as fast as possible. He was a godsend. I don't remember half of what I said, I just wanted to do what I had to do and get out of there as quickly as possible.

We have all read newspaper reports of violent crime or seen sound bites of detail on the evening news but no one can prepare you for the moment when the perpetrators describe with harrowing details, the crime they committed against someone you loved! I'll never forget the look on my grandmother's face when she heard from one of the boys involved that 'she did the dead chicken while she was dying and bleeding out on the carpet'. One of them laughed that he'd had to repeatedly kick her in the face to get her to stop.

My grandmother sat in the court, several rows behind the prosecutor's table, through the entire trial and listened to all the evidence. She listened to the gory details of how they murdered her daughter – the terror that she must have felt as she was stabbed and strangled to death in her own home, in the middle of the night by boys that she would have recognised. These were kids she had invited into her home, kids she had fed and there is no doubt she would have known who put them up to it. She died knowing her own son wanted her dead.

The matter-of-fact way they described her death was almost too much to bear. It was as if they were recounting something they had seen in a horror movie or a video game. If character is what you are in the dark then what were those boys?

If character is what you are in the dark then what was my Mom? She was a fighter and she never gave up. She fought hard for several minutes against her attackers despite being out numbered three to one, but in the end she was just no match for them. To them, she was nothing, just a thing that stood between them and what they wanted – a place to live for free and a bit of pocket money.

How wrong they were ...

They didn't see that she was a person who was deeply loved. They didn't see her strength of character and the unique and gentle way she conducted her life. My mother made a huge difference in this world. They knew nothing of the person she was and the lives that she had touched with her kindness. In the weeks after her death I received hundreds of cards from strangers, friends and neighbours. People she had helped when she worked at the hospital as the Department Head of Histology. Although she didn't need to, she would often get involved with patients, especially kids who were a little scared at having to have their blood taken and be in hospital. She would do all the procedures herself to ensure they were done quickly so as not to upset the child. She had a special way with people; putting them at ease and making them feel safe, welcome and comfortable.

They didn't see Darlene – my mother and my friend. And she didn't deserve to die.

I didn't want my brother to go to jail but I had no choice. I had to do what was right and that meant testifying against him. As Oriah Mountain Dreamer's said in her now famous poem The Invitation, *It doesn't interest me if the story you are telling me is true. I want to know if you can disappoint another to be true to yourself; if you can bear the accusation of betrayal and not betray your own soul … It doesn't interest me to know where you live or how much money you have. I want to know if you can get up, after the night of grief and despair, weary and bruised to the bone, and do what needs to be done … '.* I know there are those that felt I betrayed my brother but I did not betray my own soul and I did not betray my mother, I got up after the grief and despair, weary and bruised to the bone and did what needed to be done – however hard that was.

I have often wondered what it is that differentiates those that keep going to those that give up at the slightest challenge? Why is it that some people face backbreaking adversity and others seem to float through life unscathed? Why is it that bad things happen to good people?

I certainly don't have any definitive answer but I think 'character' is part of that equation. That invisible aspect of self that determines whether we give up or carry on. Character is something that can't be taken from us and it can't be given to us by others. It is something that is developed over time and is as obvious as the nose on your face. It is hard to define and even harder to quantify.

When I look back at my life the people that stand out for me – both good and bad – stand out because of their character or lack thereof. Those that shine like beacons of light, who demonstrate such depth of character, wisdom and love that you can't help but be in awe of their goodness. Then there are those that demonstrate no goodness, those that have been totally incapable of taking responsibility for their lives and have consistently put forward excuses and reasons to justify the unjustifiable.

No one ever said life should be easy. But having the strength to do what needs to be done no matter how difficult it gets is an essential part of life and it often comes down to character and finding a bigger more noble purpose than your individual pain. You have to keep going. You have to get back up no matter how many times you're knocked down.

There is no point 'trying', you either do or you don't. Trying is nothing more than a pre-negotiated failure. Forget 'I'll try my best', just 'Do your best'. Don't waste your time in half-hearted attempts so you can say, 'Well I tried'. Just do it – whatever *it* is.

Find a way to make the changes you dream of. Never give up. When you find yourself in the midst of extreme situations and enormous pain just keep taking baby steps. Wake up, breathe and get through one day at a time.

Things will get better but you have to make them better. You have to dig deep into your own soul and find out who you really are in the dark ... you may be astounded at how much strength you find inside and just how resourceful you can be. As Helen Keller said, *'Character cannot be developed in ease and quiet. Only through experiences of trial and suffering can the soul be strengthened, vision cleared, ambition inspired and success achieved'*.

Did you know ... ?

A great way to work out whether what you are about to do is a good thing or not is to run it through the newspaper test ... Ask yourself this question, 'If what you are about to do was to be printed on the front page of your national newspaper and broadcast around the world would you be proud or ashamed?

If the answer is that you would be ashamed, then don't do it. Character is about doing the right thing when no one is watching and if you're unsure what that is then imagine that the world is watching and make the decision you know to be right.

How to incorporate this wisdom into your life

Remove the word 'try' from your vocabulary. This would be a great thing to incorporate into your working environment. If possible, buy an air horn or a loud buzzer and tell everything that the word 'try' is no longer allowed. Any time anyone uses the word, sound the air horn! That person then must rephrase the statement without the word 'try'.

If that's a bit too radical for your liking, just do it for yourself. Inform those close to you that you are removing the word from your vocabulary and they are to remind you or point it out if they hear you using it. After a while you'll stop using it and you will either do what needs to be done or you won't. There is no middle ground. Remember the famous words of Yoda in Star Wars: 'Do or do not. There is no try'.

Chapter 31

Money is neither my god nor my devil. It is a form of energy that tends to make us more of who we already are, whether it's greedy or loving. ~ Dan Millman

Dan Millman is a former world-champion athlete, winning the 1964 World Trampoline Championships in London and co-captained the 1968 NCAA UCLA gymnastic team. He taught gymnastics at Stanford University and was the professor of physical education at Oberlin College. In his early years he also taught martial arts and was involved in modern dance. Since then he has become a key player in the field of human potential and the author of several highly regarded and successful books including his first book, a work of autobiographical fiction called *Way of the Peaceful Warrior*.

I learnt Dan Millman's truth at the hardest time of my life. After my mother was murdered, her possessions and property needed to be distributed as is the case when anyone passes away. Like most parents she had left the bulk of her assets to her children. Obviously my brother's role in her death negated any claim he had over anything. He had originally hatched the plan because he thought that he and the other boys involved would be able to stay in the house without my Mom and use the money from her insurance policy to do whatever he wanted. The boys had decided that if I objected, they would kill me next. In fact, they had a 'hit list' with about 20 names on it.

Legally (and ethically) that was never going to happen. His part in the plot and subsequent sentence ensured that he didn't receive a cent – a legal perspective that he and my father didn't necessarily agree with. I was adamant that he shouldn't benefit from the terrible thing he set in motion but at the end of the day it wasn't my choice. The law is very clear – someone charged with involvement in someone else's death can't benefit financially from that death. It's logical, perhaps even common sense, and yet that wasn't how things were viewed by some of the family.

My brother and father's sense of entitlement and hostility toward me was not a huge surprise but I was surprised by the reaction of other family members. On top of the emotional trauma that I experienced as a result of my Mom's death, the secondary grief of dealing with fallout of settling the financial affairs increased my sense of devastation. And just when I thought I had already reached rock bottom, I found that I hadn't. I learned very quickly that money can bring out either the best or the worst in people – unfortunately, it can make enemies out of friends and family very quickly.

In many ways, my mother's estate initially provided a real security blanket for me. It allowed me to purchase my first home – this allowed me to begin the re-building process which was essential for me because I felt I had lost my family and my sense of 'home' or foundation. I simply could not bear to set foot in the house where I had grown up and where she was killed. Even after the extensive clean up, the memories and the pictures that I had in my mind of what her final moments must have been like, were unbearable.

Even though the money afforded me options in terms of buying a home, affording a few luxuries and taking care of myself mentally (retreats, counselling etc), I never felt comfortable with the source of the money. To me, the money I received when her estate was finalised was dirty – I viewed it as 'blood' money. I simply wanted my Mom back. I would have done and given anything to have her back and still would. The idea that money, any sum of money, could ever compensate for the loss of a loved one is a strange and completely repugnant idea to me.

Strangely enough, members of my extended family were upset about the division of the estate – they felt that they were entitled to a portion of the proceeds and they were extremely angry and verbal about it. Instead of coming to me and discussing it directly, instead they went behind my back and talked about it to anyone else that would listen. The Crown Prosecutor, Darwin Greaves, took me aside one day to explain what was happening and to give me some valuable advice. He had become aware of what was being said by these individuals and took it upon himself to give me some fatherly (and legal) advice. I felt terrible about the whole thing and was inclined to just give everyone the amount of money they were asking for. His compassion, guidance and objectivity allowed me to withstand enormous pressure in relation to carrying out my mother's wishes on the division of her estate. And for that assistance, I am still eternally grateful.

I know that my feelings toward that inheritance contributed to the fact that it became a burden for me. I felt guilt at having it as it was only possible because my mother was dead. And yet I felt a responsibility to her to make sure that her wishes were carried out: the legal system mandated that my brother would not benefit. But the money was still tainted – just as Millman's quote points to the fact that people's intentions are what taint money, I would go one step further and say that money can also be polluted by its source.

Interestingly enough, I started my first business with the funds that I received and I honestly believe on some unconscious level that business was destined to fail because I couldn't reconcile the idea that something good could come from something so bad. I didn't actually want the money. And I certainly didn't want to benefit from it. I didn't want my life to be easier because my mother had died. In the end I lost every last cent that I received and looking back that was a huge blessing. Everything I've created for myself since has been created from hard work and a genuine desire to help others.

I never told anyone in my family that I lost the inheritance when my first business went under. Strangely enough, I continued to get requests from them for money for various reasons. There were times when they asked that I simply wasn't in a position to lend it to them. It was interesting to note their reactions. I could tell that they felt entitled to the money and extremely frustrated with me. Truth be told, if I would have had the money at the time that they asked, I probably would have lent it to them in order to pacify them. However, I didn't and I learned some very valuable lessons about who I could really count on.

Did you know ... ?

In Japan there is a special name for 'blood money' – *mimaikin*. In 2000 a British girl called Lucie Blackman was murdered in Tokyo. The leading suspect in the case was wealthy businessman Joji Obara. In 2007 Obara was jailed for life on multiple rapes charges and one manslaughter charge, however, he was acquitted of Lucie's murder. Tim Blackman, Lucie's father, had accepted £450,000 from a friend of Obara's in what is termed *mimaikin* – or condolence money. Apparently the implications of *mimaikin* are not one of guilt and it is also referred to as *tsugunaikin* or atonement money.

But does it really matter what you call it? Why would an innocent man channel the equivalent of almost $1 million dollars to the father of one of his victims if he wasn't guilty? Obara's legal team said that Mr Blackman's acceptance of this money helped their client and it is thought it played a part in ensuring he avoided the death penalty. I'm sure Mr Blackman had his reasons for accepting this money and certainly there is now a Lucie Blackman Trust dedicated to educating people on personal safety, so perhaps some good came from it after all.

Dealing with a large, unexpected sum of money (whether it be positive or negative – through a windfall, investment or inheritance) is a life-changing experience. Money can be a source of angst, resentment and hostility at the best of times, add to that the trauma and grief of an untimely death and it's a recipe for disaster!

Just look at the case of OJ Simpson. When the legal system pronounced OJ Simpson not guilty in criminal proceedings, the family of Nicole Simpson and Ron Goldman were forced to take civil action against him to ensure some form of justice was served. They won that case and OJ Simpson was ordered to pay $33.5 million to the families. He never did and instead he hid his assets.

Simpson decided to write a book called *'If I did it'* – an apparent hypothetical account of how he *would* have killed Nicole and Ron had he done it ... The fact that any publisher agreed to the book is distasteful in the extreme.

As a result, the alliance between the Brown and Goldman families split on what to do about the book. Denise Brown, Nicole's sister boycotted the book and wanted nothing to do with it, a stance that was originally shared by the Goldman family. However, the Goldman's changed their mind – they knew that Simpson would never pay the civil bill and that he had access to highly paid lawyers who would ensure he never settled the debt – either financially or spiritually. Yet they saw a way of stopping him from making the millions he would have made from the royalties. Not to mention frustrating Simpson in his attempt to make money off the notoriety and continuing to be a 'fly in his ointment'.

The Goldman family now owns the rights to Simpson's book. I'm sure it must have been a hard decision to make but left with a system that failed them at every turn, they probably felt as though they had little choice. In an interview with Oprah Winfrey, who refused to read the book and did not endorse it, Fred Goldman explained his position admirably and stressed that, 'If just one woman reads the book and recognises the signs that she is in an abusive and potentially lethal relationship and gets out it will be worth it'.

The Goldman family was able to reconcile the source of that money and channel it into something good. Nicole's family was not able to do that, and neither position is right or wrong.

The bottom line is that money is neither inherently good nor evil – it makes people more of who they really are already. It can be polluted by its source just as easily as it can be purged or blessed by that source. It's an individual experience. I couldn't come to terms with the evil that had allowed that money to exist in the first place and so I got rid of it – albeit unconsciously. For the Goldman family, they were able to find good in that evil and do what they felt needed to be done to achieve their ultimate purpose. And I admire them immensely for that.

It always comes down to how you think about money. And just as money is neither good nor bad, it is also never a valid reason for failure. Lack of money never held anyone back. As Norman Vincent Peale so rightly points out, *Empty pockets never held anyone back. Only empty heads and empty hearts can do that*. Money is simply a means to an end. Your thoughts about it – how hard it is to make, whether it's dirty, what you have to do to get it, what you intend to do with it – all have the power to influence your ultimate results.

Money is as necessary in this world as oxygen, but it doesn't play favourites, and despite the fact that the divide between the rich and poor appears to increase it is not a fast track to happiness or fulfilment. I have met miserable millionaires and people with very little who exude contentment and love. On one hand, if you use money or the lack thereof as a justification for inactivity and a reason why you are unsuccessful then you as destined to stay in that situation. On the other, if you make money your god and pursue it relentlessly as the expense of everything and everybody then you will eventually pay the price. Money is meaningless in and of itself. Everything it represents is injected by us. Whether it is a force for good and a motivation for greater achievement or a product of ill-gotten gain is entirely down to the meaning we ascribe.

How to incorporate this wisdom into your life

Money is very often tangled up with misconceptions and assumptions that change the way we see it. Working out what your unconscious beliefs and values are about money can be very illuminating. Get a clean sheet of paper – ask and answer the following six questions over and over again until you run out of replies. Once you think you don't have anything left to say about money, make yourself find five more answers – these will probably be some of your most meaningful and insightful responses!

1. People with money are?
2. Money is?
3. Money is good because?
4. Money is bad because?
5. Rich people are?
6. Money is important to me – for what purpose?

Whether we have money or not, or can do something positive with money or not, depends solely on our perceptions of it. If we view money as a means to an end and a way to effect change or make a positive difference in the world, then we are much more likely to possess enough of it to achieve our dreams (as opposed to if we believe that all rich people are crooks and that there is nobility in poverty).

Chapter 32

The Maxim 'Nothing avails but perfection' may be spelled 'Paralysis' ~ Winston Churchill

Winston Churchill was perhaps one of the most outstanding politicians of the 20th century. He was the prime minister of Great Britain during the Second World War and again from 1951–1955. Churchill was a master statesman, orator and strategist and his leadership was without question instrumental in winning the war. Churchill was also an officer in the British Army. He was also a prolific author and won the Nobel Prize in Literature in 1953 for his historical writings. Churchill was known for his sharp wit and is one of the most often quoted men in history. One of my other personal favourites is – 'A lie gets halfway around the world before the truth has a chance to get its pants on!'

The process of writing this book has been an emotional and difficult journey at times. Reviewing memories and thoughts long buried has meant that I have spent many hours in floods of tears as I remember people and events from the past.

The process has been a revelation and has illustrated to me just how bound up in perfection I can often get. At one point toward the end of the project I became completely overwhelmed. All I could see was what was wrong with the manuscript, commas in the wrong place, little spelling mistakes and sections yet to be completed. It seemed like an endless task that stretched out in front of me and I was engulfed with trepidation.

Luckily I had someone on the outside to help me to gain a more objective perspective and to realise that what I saw as 'faults' were not necessarily important at that point in the process. I was so hung up on perfection that I was literally being paralysed by it.

As I took a few deep breaths and continued I was able to see just how toxic this idea of perfection is and has been all my life. For the most part I am deeply grateful for my drive and persistence to make things better and to improve but there is a point beyond which that trait is clearly unhelpful.

Perfectionism has, over the years, produced deeply felt anxiety and has on occasion manifested in panic attacks. My parents, especially my Dad, expected a great deal from me. As I mentioned in Chapter 3, I was enrolled in private figure skating lessons, piano and ballet when I was just six years old. My days would often start at 5 am with ice skating lessons at 6 am and my evenings and weekends were a constant round of skating, ballet classes and piano practice and that was even before I got to my school homework. When it came to ice skating I did have a natural talent and ability but I feel sure that this relentless pursuit of perfection was detrimental to my performance. I vividly remember being humiliated in front of my peers and my coach as my Dad shouted at me for not performing to his exacting standards. I don't know if it was partly because I was the first child or he wanted to live out his dreams through me but I was certainly pushed rather than encouraged!

Things got so bad that I began to dread going to the rink. I was so terrified of doing poorly and yet I was never really praised or rewarded when I did excel. There was never any carrot, only a stick, and that has had a profound impact on my life. When your very best effort is never good enough it can be soul destroying for anyone – especially a child.

Conversely my brother was never pushed to pursue anything as a young child. I never understood that disparity although I think it had something to do with a health scare when he was very young. As an infant he was given the usual inoculations but he had a reaction to them, became very sick and was hospitalised. I was only seven at the time and I still remember it very clearly in my mind – I went with my parents to the hospital, the doctors and nurses were scrambling around and my parents were worried that he might not make it. There was little we could do except wait and I remember being terrified that he might die and not come home ever again. I often wonder if the scare of almost losing him meant they didn't want to put so much pressure on him.

If you present symptoms of depression, addictions or stress and anxiety it can usually be traced back to events in early life. The thought-feeling reactions created when you experience emotionally charged events over the course of your life form a chain of events – much like a string of pearls. The string is essentially created from the initial sensitising event (or 'ISE') to each of the subsequent events that reinforce those particular thoughts, emotions and feelings. The ability to trace back through your past to the first time you experienced the problem can break the thought-feeling connection and is the key to eliminating the problem and the symptoms forever. Age regression and time line therapy are both effective tools for identifying the ISE and breaking the thought-feeling connection. When I experienced this for the first time I was able to see the initial events and all the subsequent reinforcing events throughout my life.

For example, I was able to identify hundreds of times that I felt extreme anxiety and panic. As a young child, around the age of eight or nine, I was often left at home alone in the evenings while my parents ran errands. I was left with chores to do – vacuuming, tidying up etc – and my parents would take my baby brother with them. As the evening progressed, it became dark outside and panic would set in. I would turn on all the lights in the house in order to feel safe and I would shut the door to the basement – I wouldn't go down there by myself when I was alone and it was dark outside. I would try to keep myself as busy as possible in order to keep my mind off the fact that I felt alone and terrified.

Some nights I would call my grandparents on the phone and they would stay on the line with me for hours, just talking, until I saw the lights of my parent's car pull up in the driveway. I didn't understand why I had been left at home alone. As soon as I saw the lights in the driveway, I would hang up the phone, run upstairs and jump into bed to pretend that I was sleeping. I wasn't allowed to tell anyone, including grandma and grandpa, that I had been left alone. If my dad found out that I was on the phone with them, I was punished severely for telling and for 'being a baby'. Ironically, I think I was more afraid of him than being alone in the dark. All of these situations just affirmed my existing anxiety so when I was finally able to release those emotions through time line and thought field therapy (TFT) it was incredibly liberating.

The skills and character traits that I developed though being pushed as a youngster have in many ways proved very useful as an adult. I have discovered abilities and talents I may never have uncovered but every coin has two sides – in this case fear and encouragement – and using fear as the sole source of motivation is never effective. It can be a powerful

Did you know ... ?

Like many personality traits, perfectionism tends to run in families and probably has a genetic component. Parents who have an authoritarian style combined with conditional love may contribute to perfectionism in their children. It is likely that the child learnt early in life that they were mainly valued for their achievements. This may or may not have been true, but the result was the same if that was the youngster's interpretation. As a result the child may have learned to value themselves only on the basis of other people's approval.

As a result, self-esteem may be based primarily on external standards and this can leave the individual vulnerable and sensitive to the opinions and criticism of others. Perfectionism is therefore created as a good defence.

In trying to understand the pros and cons of perfectionist behaviour, Robert B Slaney, a counselling psychologist in Penn State's College of Education created the Almost Perfect scale, which contains four variables: Standards and Order, Relationships, Anxiety, and Procrastination.

This can be a useful way of looking at your drive for perfection. If it allows you to create standards and orders that assist you in consistent performance then it's a positive form. If, however, it causes you to put unreal expectations on others and therefore avoid meaningful relationships then it's not helpful. The same is true if your drive for perfection causes abnormal anxiety and stops you from getting into action.

counterpoint but only when it's balanced with the possibility of reward and encouragement.

As we discussed in Chapter 5, toward motivation (rather than away motivation) is always much more powerful and effectual in the long term. Who knows what I might have achieved in my skating career if I had simply been encouraged to just enjoy it, have fun and do the best I could instead of feeling trapped and scared of the consequences should I fail? As Napoleon Bonaparte said, *'There are two levers for moving men – interest and fear'*. Using one at the expense of the other is never as effective as using both together.

Being a parent must be the hardest job in the world … finding a balance between encouraging your children to find their own way and being the best they can be and erring on the side of being a bully! I honestly think for the most part my Dad's intentions were good – he just wanted me to do well but his way of showing that left a lot to be desired. Thankfully, I no longer suffer from panic and severe anxiety. With the lessons and insights that I have learned along the way, many of which I have shared with you in this book, I have managed to heal myself and not let it rule my life or prevent me from action.

I sometimes have to remind myself that perfection is impossible. We can only ever do the best we can do in any given moment with the resources and knowledge we have at that time. I have no doubt that in years to come I will read this book again and wish I'd said things differently or find chapters I could have improved, but that is life. There comes a time in every life and in every project when you need to come to the decision that your absolute best is good enough. Otherwise you stay on the sidelines making excuses for why you can't just make things happen because, 'it wasn't quite good enough'. Putting everything you have into something and actually doing it, even if it's imperfect is always superior to endless talk, no action and perfection paralysis. A drive for constant improvement is always an admirable trait when coupled with action but otherwise it's debilitating.

And what is perfect anyway? Who defines it? I know, for example, that there will be people who read this book and absolutely love it, it will resonate with them and it's my deepest hope that it will allow a new perspective to flourish that assists readers all over the world. I also, rather reluctantly, concede that there will be people that hate it. I can't control that, I have to let it go and accept, as French writer Alfred De Musset said, *'Perfection does not exist. To understand that is the triumph of human intelligence; to expect to possess it is the most dangerous kind of madness'*.

How to incorporate this wisdom into your life

If you consider the Pareto principal, which states that 20% of your effort is responsible for 80% of your results, it follows that the remaining 80% of effort produces a minuscule 20% of your results.

Try spending the 20% to get your efforts to 80% perfect. That is your goal. Don't start with a goal that requires perfection. Once your project or task is 80% finished leave it for a few days and tackle and allocate a deadline where your effort, however close to perfect, must be complete. Practice accepting your best given the factors relevant to each situation. You might be surprised to find out that your 80% is still better than many people's 100%!

Conclusion

Grant me the serenity to accept the things I cannot change; the courage to change the things I can; and the wisdom to know the difference. ~ St Francis of Assisi

St Francis of Assisi was a Roman Catholic friar who lived between 1118 and 1226. He was the founder of the Order of Friars Minor known as the Franciscans and is the patron saint of animals, birds and the environment!

Known as the serenity prayer, this statement from one of history's great giants probably appears on millions of fridges the world over. Mouse pads, calendars and screen savers remind us of the sentiment on a fairly regular basis. Consequently its relevance and importance can often be cast aside in our familiarity.

Yet what is the truth of life? Where do we so often pour our energy and focus? Into the very things we cannot change. We commonly display no commitment or determination to change the things we can and are forever confusing the two!

When Michael Milton lost his leg to cancer when he was nine, he and his parents could have decided that his life was over. It would have been perfectly understandable for him to feel sorry for himself and withdrawn from the activities he loved and become a victim of his misfortune. But he didn't.

Instead he became a Paralympics Gold Medal Ski champion. A feat in itself but he has also climbed the world's highest free standing mountain with his sister. As anyone who has actually reached the summit of Kilimanjaro will tell you that is an incredible accomplishment. Kili is 19,340 feet high and claims more lives than any other mountain. Only 20% of those who start the climb make it to the top. Sub zero temperatures and the unpredictability of altitude sickness make Kili a Mecca for adventurers the world over. Michael Milton had one leg.

He accepted the things he could not change – the amputation of his leg through cancer. He displayed the courage to change the things he could and learned how to adapt to his new situation. And he had the wisdom to know the difference. He didn't waste time wallowing in self-pity. I'm sure there were times he did feel sorry for himself, I'm sure there were times he was angry at why it had happened to him, but he didn't *live* in those emotions. Instead he poured all his focus on what he could change and achieved amazing things despite his disability, not because of it.

For me, I couldn't change the fact that my mother was dead. I couldn't bring her back and I couldn't change the fact that my brother was responsible. But that realisation didn't come easy. Initially I couldn't accept the things I couldn't change, instead I spent years searching for a 'sign', soliciting advice, angling for approval, demanding justification and answers about why this happened to me, seeking guarantees and longing just to belong to something or someone. My refusal to accept the things I couldn't change, and persistent drive to ignore the things I could change resulted in physical illness, stress and debilitation that escalated sufficiently to gain my undivided attention. One thing I have learned in my life is that the size of the lesson is always directly proportionate to the size of the piece of wood that the universe has to hit me with in order to get my attention.

I spent a lot of time and energy fighting battles I could not win, resisting events or circumstances I could not change, trying to influence decisions that had already been made and trying to prevent the inevitable. I saw myself as the victim and I identified with that feeling of powerlessness at the very core of my being. I hated what had happened but somehow I was also scared and reluctant to let it go and move on with my life. All the victim support groups and psychotherapy in the world could not help me – they only served to further entrench the negative feelings and sense of helplessness. I began to realise that I needed to make significant changes within myself.

Life's many lessons have taught me that while I am absolutely at cause for every event I have experienced or attracted into my life, once it has happened, there is nothing that I can do to change it in the past. The point of power is 'now' and it is all in my own mind. I may not be able to change the event but I do have the power to change its meaning. I can choose to attribute a meaning and adopt an attitude that supports and empowers me toward a compelling future. Or I can remain a prisoner of the past and adopt an attitude of a victim devoid of hope and possibilities.

The only thing we have absolute control over is our own mind – our ability to choose our own way. Even in the face of unbelievable atrocities, hope and love are possible if we plant the right seeds in our minds.

By standing on the shoulders of giants I was able to reframe in my mind the meanings that I gave to various significant events in my life. Instead of looking at my mother's death as the end of my world, I began to view it as an indication of a bright future. I am encouraged by Laurens Van du Post's quote, *'The depth of darkness to which you can descend and still live is an exact measure of the height to which you can aspire to reach'*.

You see I have a distinct advantage over many others because I have already lived through the worst experience of my life and I survived. So I know with an absolute conviction that I am strong enough to handle anything life brings my way.

I have embraced St Francis of Assisi's words. I have accepted the things I cannot change; I have showed courage to change the things I can and I fully understand the difference. I think my Mom would be proud.

References
Suggested Further Reading

1. C. Howard, *Results Certification Training Manual*, 2006, pp 7.1-7.3.
2. R. Diekstra, *Haarlemmer Dagblad*, 1993, cited by L. Derks & J. Hollander, *Essenties van NLP* (Utrecht: Servire, 1996), p 58.
3. Anthony Robbins, *Awaken the Giant Within*, pp 207, 208, 211.
4. John David Hoag, *The Map is Not The Territory*, Website article at www.nlpls.com, 2007, p 1.
5. Bill Bryson, *Mother Tongue*, p 3.
6. Michael Talbot, *Holographic Universe*, p 102.
7. Morris Massey, *The People Puzzle*, 1979, p 8-23.
8. Kimberly dela Cruz Odom, Article at www.thinque.com.au/assets/whatdoyou.pdf, pp 1-2.
9. Website – Christopherreeve.org
10. Alive: The Andes Accident 1972 – Official website.
11. Michael Talbot, *The Holographic Universe*, p 3.
12. Dr Deepak Chopra, *Destiny: Harnessing the infinite power of coincidence to create miracles*, pp 121, 124, 125.
13. Lawrence Tabak, If Your Goal is Success, Don't Consult These Gurus, Dec 1996.
14. Stanley, Thomas (2004) *Millionaire Women Next Door*.
15. Anthony Robbins, *Awaken the Giant Within*, p 38.
16. Jack Canfield and Mark Victor Hanson, *Chicken Soup for the Soul*, p 228.
17. Harald Anderson, *A Motivational Story with Wisdom – Be Realistic: Create a Miracle!*, 2004.
18. Website – Wikipedia, Mohamed Ali, *Rumble in the Jungle*.
19. Website – Wikipedia, Wayne Gretzky.
20. Joseph Campbell, *The Power of Myth*, pp 113, 120.
21. Joseph Campbell Foundation website.
22. Stanislav Grof, *The Adventures of Self-Discovery, Dimensions of consciousness and new perspectives in psychology and inner exploration*, p 152.
23. Steve Young, *Great Failures of the Extremely Successful*, p 115.
24. Robert Fulgrum, *All I Really Needed to Know I Learned in Kindergarten*, 2004, p 2.

25. Stanislav Grof, *The Adventures of Self-Discovery, Dimensions of consciousness and new perspectives in psychology and inner exploration*, p 90.

26. Harriet Rubin, *What Is Courage?* (www.fastcompany.com), Issue 55, Jan 2002, p 96.

27. Galen Guengerich, *Cadence of Courage, A sermon by*, New York Sept 16, 2006.

28. Jonathan Marx, *Ometz Lev – Courage*, (www.ashrei.com/ometzlev. htm).

29. Michael Talbot, *Holographic Universe*, pp 88, 93, 94, 220.

30. *What the Bleep Do We Know – Down the Rabbit Hole* 5 DVD collection, DVD 2.

31. Rocco Oppedisano, *A Guide To Memory Increase*, 1991, Chapter 8.

32. Robert Cialdini, *Influence Science and Practice*.

33. Tian Dayton, *The Magic of forgiveness: Emotional Freedom and Transformation at Midlife*, 2003.

34. Mark Liberman, *Etymology As Argument*, June 18, 2005.

35. Mary Bryant, *Reconciliation and forgiveness www.unija.org*, 21 June 2006.

36. Dr Wayne Dyer's website www.drwaynedyer.com.

37. Anthony Robbins, *Personal Power CD series,* Disk 4, tracks 2 and 3.

38. Michael Talbot, *Holographic Universe*, p 101.

39. Maxwell Maltz, *Pyscho Cybernetics*, 1960.

Appendix I
About The Author

Rhondalynn has a creative and inspiring story that proves that you can **BE, DO** and **HAVE** anything you set your mind to. From humble beginnings and despite formidable obstacles, to success as a leader and entrepreneur, Rhondalynn is one of the most dynamic and inspiring speakers on the power of communication, influence and the science of the self-image.

A 16-year veteran of sales, marketing and finance, Rhondalynn holds degrees and professional designations in law and chartered accounting and she is a certified Master Practitioner of NLP, Thought Field Therapist, Clinical Hypnotherapist and Psychotherapist. Her CV features an impressive list of accomplishments in senior executive positions with Macleod Dixon, Price Waterhouse Coopers, Max Factor, Covergirl, Village Cinemas, FlyBuys and Coles Group Ltd.

Her methodologies are engaging and memorable -- she physically demonstrates the mind/body link and proves the power of re-writing negative conditioning, goal setting and creative visualization. She has a natural ability to motivate, lead and empower others to unlock and achieve their full potential. Combining intellect, intuition, innovation, insight and integrity, her work reveals the limitless possibilities that are made available when you connect with the infinite resourcefulness of the subconscious mind. She has been featured in national business publications and on radio across North America and Australia.

Rhondalynn speaks annually to thousands of entrepreneurs, sales professionals, senior executives, franchisees, sporting clubs, corporate employees and industry association members on the principles of success, leadership, business acceleration, peak performance and mental toughness.

As an entrepreneur, Rhondalynn founded Imagineering Unlimited in to serve the growing demand for customized training, consulting and results coaching solutions based on leading edge, scientifically proven technologies. That mission is realized via transformational events, seminars, training and coaching curriculums that ignite the quest for self mastery while offering practical and proven techniques to rise above challenges and realize your deepest dreams and potential.

Get To Know Rhondalynn

Follow Rhondalynn on Twitter - http://twitter.com/Rhondalynn

Become a fan of "On The Shoulders of Giants" on Facebook

Visit Rhondalynn's Blog at www.imagineeringunlimited.com

Appendix II
Taking The Next Step...

Did you know:

- 97.5% of people quit smoking, start again
- 95% of people who diet, gain the weight back
- 97% of people leave one relationship, only to end up in the same situation with their next partner

Why do we keep repeating the same self sabotaging behaviour over and over again in our lives? Are we unwell, somehow deficient or addictive personalities? WHY on earth would we want to sabotage ourselves? That's a complicated question with a very simple answer... **Because our minds are wired that way: Sabotage is an automatic response of the subconscious mind.**

As you have learned, the subconscious mind cannot think and it does not know the difference between a real or imagined experience. The subconscious is very powerful & it can only **ACT** or **CREATE** based upon what is perceived to be of value. That value is determined by our experiences and conditioning over a lifetime – every event that we have encountered and what we have chosen to make that mean.

Where there is incongruence between conscious thought and what we think we deserve or think is possible (subconsciously), sabotage will prevent us from achieving our desired outcomes. The good news is that these unproductive habits and patterns of negative thinking and conditioning can be re-written – in fact, self sabotage is reversible!

Want to Get Rid of Self Sabotage And Attract More of What You Want?

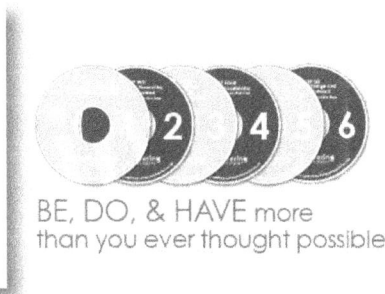

BE, DO, & HAVE more
than you ever thought possible

The processes I use to elicit deep change and lasting results are based on my own experiences, modern day science and ancient wisdom. I too am standing on the shoulders of giants so that I can offer you the tools you need to find your true intention, purpose and meaning and to make changes to your unconscious default settings and achieve your heart's desire.

Imagineering Your Destiny is a highly effective and proven tool which gives every person the capacity to re-write negative conditioning and self sabotage patterns in order to enjoy high self-image. Over 28 days, for just 30 minutes a day, this revolutionary 6 CD program promotes the self-image by combining the crucial elements of goal setting, guided relaxation, creative visualisation and repetitive auto-suggestion in order to promote rapid results, lasting success and sustained motivation. You will discover the tools and the mindset you need to re-write negative conditioning from the past, move beyond perceived limitations and beginning living the life you were meant to live.

It has been scientifically proven that our brain circuits take engrams or memory traces, and produce neuro connections only if they are bombarded with the information for 21 days in a row. This means that our brain does not accept 'new' data or habit changes unless they are repeated each day for **at least 21 days, without missing a day.**

The process is extremely easy and relaxing – you will be fully aware of the suggestions being made for the promotion of your improved self image and success.

CD 1 - Step One: Relaxation and Healing (5 days)
CD 2 - Step Two: Unlocking the Power of the Subconscious Mind (5 days)
CD 3 - Step Three: Re-Building the Self Image (5 days)
CD 4 - Step Four: Attraction Accelerator (5 days)
CD 5 - Step Five: Questions Are The Answers... (4 days)
CD 6 - Step Six: Open to Change and Moving Forward (4 days)

Imagineering Your Destiny is based on the principles and philosophies of the science of self-image reprogramming first pioneered by Dr. Maxwell Maltz in the 1960's. This revolutionary audio program is based on my cumulative experience and expertise as a Clinical Hypnotherapist, Psychotherapist, Thought Field Therapist, Master Practitioner of NLP and Master Results coach – working with individuals, groups and organizations around the world.

Now, for the first time, I am making a digitally mastered version available - now YOU can enjoy this life changing program, no matter where you live!

Discover How *Imagineering Your Destiny* Can Help You Change Your Life!

I believe we all deserve to live inspired, abundant and purposeful lives, regardless of our upbringing or the significant emotional events that we have encountered in the past. *Imagineering Your Destiny* is about re-connecting to your dreams and re-engineering your destiny. *Imagineering Your Destiny* will allow you to create a vision that is so real, vibrant and compelling that you cannot continue to merely sleep through your life. It's a wake-up call of monumental proportions – to open your eyes and realise that you can see, do and have more than you ever thought possible.

Visit the website today – I have prepared a FREE video to explain clearly how *Imagineering Your Destiny* works and allow you to take your first step toward becoming even more successful NOW!

www.imagineeringunlimited.com/destiny

Here's What Clients Are Saying About *Imagineering Your Destiny*

"The program has enabled me to develop a far more positive attitude and clarity around my goals. The regular use of this program has increased my confidence, eliminated anxiety and enhanced my creativity and vision."
Teresa Foti, Entrepreneur

"In business and in life, it is all about attitude and mindset. What I think becomes my reality. This program has been an incredible boost to the strategies that I picked up in my coaching sessions and I would recommend it without hesitation to anyone who is serious about taking their results and success to the next level!"
Marnie Browne, Fem Skin Therapy

"The skill sets and methodologies in this program are first rate and Rhondalynn has a proven track record for unleashing potential (both in individuals and organizations) and delivering incremental results quickly and easily."
Mario Ragusa, Intellectual Property Development Director

"My panic attacks and headaches came to a complete stop. My energy level has gone from a 1 to a 100. I think more clearly, I feel great about myself and accomplish so much every day. I make decisions easily now and don't have to think about them forever! I am doing more and thinking less. My negative thoughts have disappeared... my self esteem has soared and I'm not afraid to try things. I feel settled and that my life has purpose again... AND it's only been 3 weeks since I began using the program! My focus in life has completely changed - I now know what I want and I am going out and getting it !!"
Shelley Brandt Merhi, Entrepreneur

BE, DO, & HAVE more
than you ever thought possible

www.imagineeringunlimited.com/destiny

Appendix III
More On The Shoulders of Giants?

Would you like to be part of **On The Shoulders of Giants** Volume 2? Share your inspiring story of how you (or your loved ones) have stood on the shoulders of giants to triumph over adversity, move beyond your past and perceived limitations, overcome your fears, find love, make a lifestyle change, start a new career, kick an unproductive/destructive habit, become more loving and forgiving or even become a "magnet" for attracting everything you DO want!

Please send us your stories, poems, articles, photos – anything you feel would inspire and empower others to embrace the profound wisdom of the many giants in our world - everyday heroes or philosophical/famous giants who have profoundly touched your life and changed its course forever. And remember, each one of us has within us the potential and the power to be a true giant in the lives of others – never underestimate the capacity for a kind word or a smile to move mountains, re-define what is possible or change a life. You are already amazing and I encourage you to continue to share your unique gifts, talents and insights!

Email us now at: info@imagineeringunlimited.com

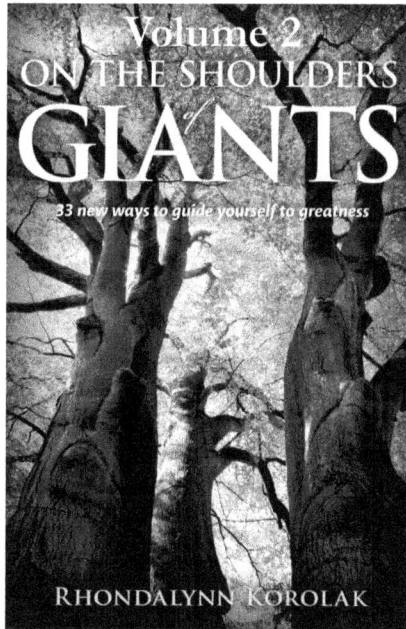

Appendix IV
Please Visit Our Website

www.imagineeringunlimited.com

to receive:

- Your **FREE copy** of our Enewsletter – packed full of insightful tips and strategies, Q&A from readers around the world and powerful, inspiring case stories of readers who have used the tools to put the past and perceived limitations behind them once and for all and create the life of their dreams
- Special VIP offers (available online only) for members – including pre-release pricing on ALL upcoming products
- Exclusive audio and video tools to help you become even more successful today
- Access to Rhondalynn's blog and highlights from her radio interviews
- Advance notice of all events and Rhondalynn's appearances coming soon to a city near you!

Thank you for becoming part of the Imagineering Unlimited community and for allowing us the privilege of partnering with you to share and build upon the wisdom of everyday heroes and giants around the world. May the light of WHO you really are shine bright and strong through your words, decisions and actions.

Rhondalynn